CONTENTS

Ships in Focus Publications
Correspondence and editorial:
Roy Fenton
18 Durrington Avenue
London SW20 8NT
020 8879 3527
rfenton@rfenton.demon.co.uk

Orders and photographic:
John & Marion Clarkson
18 Franklands, Longton
Preston PR4 5PD
01772 612855
sales@shipsinfocus.co.uk

Printed by Amadeus Press Ltd., Cleckheaton, Yorkshire.
Designed by Hugh Smallwood, John Clarkson and Roy Fenton.
SHIPS IN FOCUS RECORD
ISBN 1 901703 20 7

SHIPS IN FOC

Marc

In this issue we begin a history b built for charter to the nationalised British steel industry. Now ore carriers may not be the sexiest ships for most enthusiasts, but John's history is fascinating, not least because it debunks the received wisdom that nationalised industries are not innovative. Here we see a state-owned enterprise radically reforming its ore delivering operations, and having a vision of the future shipment of this commodity which has helped develop the ore and bulk carriers of today. John's articles describe the birth of the project, move on to consider how it worked in practice, take a hard look at its results, and discuss how a number of the carriers were radically rebuilt in later life. Alongside his chapters, we are presenting his list of these ore carriers, fully illustrated, in several parts. We are particularly proud to publish such a well-researched, well-written and original feature: articles like this are one of the reasons we started *Record.*

Not for the first time, writing captions for a feature in *Record* (this time on Finnish veterans still sailing in the fifties) has reconfirmed the value of the Starke/Schell series of registers. These invaluable volumes list each ship built in a given year, along with key dimensions, histories and fates. Registers for many of the years between 1890 and 1984 have been produced, and are being published by the World Ship Society. The latest list of those available, including electronic versions, appeared in the February 2003 issue of the Society's journal *Marine News.* Those without access to this are invited to contact us at our London address for details of the large and growing range of registers issued.

Lastly, an apology. *Record* is usually sent out to customers during the first weekend of every third month, March, June, September and December. This March it will be a little late, largely because of holidays. But we assure you, its contents will not date, and it's well worth waiting for. As will be the June issue, in which we will include a colour section as well as eight bonus pages.

John Clarkson Roy Fenton

SUBSCRIPTION RATES FOR RECORD

Subscribers make a saving on postage, and receive each *Record* just as soon as it is published. They are also eligible for concessions on newly-published *Ships in Focus* titles. Readers can start their subscription with *any* issue, and are welcome to backdate it to receive previous issues.

	3 issues	**6 issues**	**9 issues**
UK	£23	£44	£63
Europe (airmail)	£25	£47	£68
Rest of world (surface mail)	£25	£47	£68
Rest of world (airmail)	£30	£56	£81

Riding light, the ore carrier *Redcar* is at anchor apparently unballasted. A major series on the BISCO ore carriers begins on page 164. *[J. and M. Clarkson]*

Venus (2) of 1931 as rebuilt following the Second World War.

BY BERGEN LINE FROM NEWCASTLE Part 2

Anthony Cooke

Mercur above, in her elegant original incarnation, and below at Bergen on 26th June 1933 looking a much more staid old lady after re-engining and a certain amount of rebuilding.
[Above: F.W. Hawks]

Fleet list

All vessels are steel and single screw unless stated.

MERCUR 1889-1939 Iron and steel
972g 614n 207.0 x 29.7 x 21.5 feet.
C. 2-cyl. by Lindholmens Verk., Gothenburg; 169 NHP.
1921: T. 3-cyl. built by Akers Mek. Verksted, Christiania in 1900.
5.1883: Completed by Motola Mek. Verkstads, Gothenburg (Yard No. 382) for Det Søndenfjelds-Norske D/S, Christiania as KONG DAG.
8.1889: Acquired by Det Bergenske Dampskibsselskab, Bergen and renamed MERCUR.
1902: Reboilered.
1906 and *1919*: Grounded.
1921: Re-engined.
1.1939: Sold and converted to a lighter. Later owned by Christiania-Portland Cementfabrik as ELSE.
1952: Broken up.

N.B. Some sources claim that the *Mercur* was still sailing in 1950 when she foundered during a storm in the Mediterranean while under Israeli ownership. According to 'Lloyd's Register', this was another *Mercur* (844 gross tons, built 1901 by Fyenoord of Rotterdam, ex-*Falkenstein*, ex-*Diana*) which had recently been sold by the Danish company Dampskibsselskab af 1925 to Israeli owners.

NEPTUN 1890-1928
959g 597n 198.4 x 30.3 x 13.2 feet.
1904: 1,098g 680n 218.8 x 30.0 x 13.2 feet.
T. 3-cyl. by A.G. H. Pauksch, Landsberg; 220 NHP.
6.1890: Completed by J. C. Tecklenborg, Geestemünde (Yard No. 131) for Det Bergenske Dampskibsselskab, Bergen as NEPTUN.
1904: Lengthened by Bergens Mek. Verks, Bergen.
4.1928: Broken up by Stavanger Skipsophugning Co. at Stavanger.

MIRA 1891-1941
996g 579n 202.2 x 30.2 x 15.1 feet.
1907: 1,112g 685n 221.7 x 30.2 x 15.1 feet
T.3-cyl. by A. & J. Inglis, Glasgow.
6.1891: Completed by A. & J. Inglis, Glasgow (Yard No. 219) for Det Bergenske Dampskibsselskab, Bergen as MIRA.
1907: Lengthened.
4.3.1941: Captured and sunk by the destroyer HMS BEDOUIN whom she encountered south east of Brettesnesnakken, Norway prior to the Lofoten Raid. MIRA was on a voyage from Svolvaer to Narvik with passengers and general cargo.

VENUS (1)/SYLVIA 1893-1933
1,067g 627n 230 .7 x 31.2 x 11. 9 feet.
T. 3-cyl by Wallsend Slipway Co. Ltd., Wallsend-on-Tyne.
3.1890: Completed by C. S. Swan & Hunter, Newcastle-upon-Tyne (Yard No. 153). Laid up when original owners defaulted on payment.
1893: Acquired by Det Bergenske Dampskibsselskab, Bergen as VENUS.
1903: Reboilered.
1930: Renamed SYLVIA, ceding her original name to the line's new flagship.
9.1933: Scrapped by Brodrene Anda at Stavanger.

Top: *Neptun* of 1890.
[Sammlung Siersdorfer 218/42A]
Middle: *Mira* of 1891.
[Sammlung Siersdorfer 172/16]
Bottom: *Venus* (1) of 1893. *[F.W. Hawks]*

VEGA (1) 1895-1916
1,164g 739n 233.2 x 32.1 x 12. 4 feet.
T. 3-cyl. by J. Dickinson, Sunderland; 222 NHP.
5.1895: Completed by Joseph L. Thompson and Sons Ltd., Sunderland (Yard No. 327) for Det Bergenske Dampskibsselskab, Bergen as VEGA.
1909: Reboilered.
17.11.1916: Captured, shelled and sunk by the German submarine U 78 in a position 24 miles south west of Haaboen whilst on a voyage from Bergen and Stavanger to Newcastle-upon-Tyne with passengers and canned goods.

IRMA 1905-1944
1,299g 736n 244.0 x 32.8 x 13.3 feet.
T. 3-cyl. by J. Dickinson and Son Ltd., Sunderland; 243 NHP.
4.1905: Completed by Sir Raylton Dixon and Co. Ltd., Middlesbrough (Yard No. 510) for Det Bergenske Dampskibsselskab, Bergen as IRMA.
13.2.1944: Torpedoed and sunk by the Norwegian MTB 627 and MTB 633 off Hustadvika, near Hestskjaer whilst on a voyage from Ålesund to Kristiansund with general cargo and passengers.

Upper: *Vega* (1).
[Sammlung Siersdorfer 218/1]

Lower: *Irma.*
[Sammlung Siersdorfer 218/2]

Jupiter (1) is seen, top and middle, in Bergen Line colours, and bottom in Greek ownership as *Hermes* in 1959. The changes are not just cosmetic: the well deck forward of her bridge has been filled in. *[Top: F.W. Hawks; middle A. Duncan; bottom J. and M. Clarkson]*

JUPITER (1) 1916-1955
2,506 915n 305.4 x 41.5 x 18.1 feet.
T. 3-cyl. by Lindholmens Verkstads A/B, Gothenburg.
11.9.1915: Launched by Lindholmens Verkstads A/B, Gothenburg (Yard No. 423) for Det Bergenske Dampskibsselskab, Bergen as JUPITER.
1.1916: Completed.
1917: Chartered by the Shipping Controller, London and placed under the British flag.
24.4.1918 to *8.12.1918:* Managers Union-Castle Mail Steamship Co. Ltd., London.
1.1919: Returned to Det Bergenske Dampskibsselskab, Bergen.
8.1940: Requisitioned by German forces at Copenhagen.
6.1945: Liberated at Copenhagen and returned to Det Bergenske Dampskibsselskab, Bergen.
3.1946: Returned to service.
9.1955: Sold to Epirotiki Steamship Navigation Co. 'George Potamianos' S.A., Piraeus and converted into a cruise ship, renamed HERMES.
4.3.1960: Caught fire while refitting at Perama, and beached at Sileniai Bay, Salamis.
3.9.1960: Refloated, and sold to Italian shipbreakers who resold her to Brodospas, Split.

LEDA (1) 1920-1945
2,520g 1,121n 305.6 x 41.7 x 18.4 feet.
High pressure and low pressure turbines, double-reduction geared to a single screw, by Wallsend Slipway Co. Ltd., Wallsend-on-Tyne.
11.1920: Completed by Sir W. G. Armstrong, Whitworth and Co. Ltd., Newcastle-upon-Tyne (Yard No. 965) for Det Bergenske Dampskibsselskab, Bergen as LEDA.
7.1940: Requisitioned by Germany and used as an escort vessel.
25.3.1945: Sunk by Russian field artillery near Gross Siegendorff whilst on a voyage from Stettin to Swinemünde.
12.1948: Refloated.
26.1.1949: Arrived Lübeck.
16.12.1949: Left for Bremerhaven.
9.1.1950: Sold to Eisen und Stahl A.G. and broken up at Bremerhaven.

Two views of the first *Leda* in Bergen Line ownership, the busy scene at Bergen below being on 26th June 1933. *[Samlung Siersdorfer 218/3]*

Leda (1) in the German Navy in some interesting dazzle paint: note the effect at the bow. She is described as a Sicherheitschiff, or safety vessel. *[Sammlung Siersdorfer 218/13A]*

VENUS (2) 1931-1968 Twin screw
5,407g 2,867n (412.0) 398.5 x 54.2 x 26.6 feet.
5.1948: 6,272g 3,521n (420.5) 406.4 x 54.2 x 26.6 feet.
Two 10-cyl. 4SCSA oil engines by Burmeister & Wain, Copenhagen driving twin screws; 1,190 NHP.
29.4.1931: Delivered by Helsingørs Jernskibs & Maskinbyggeri, Helsingør (Yard No. 198) to Det Bergenske Dampskibsselskab, Bergen as VENUS.
6.5.1931: Entered service.
9.1939: Laid up in Osterfjorden at the outbreak of war.
16.3.1941: Requisitioned by Germany.
20.3.1945: Sunk by Allied aircraft at Hamburg.
9.1945: Raised and later towed to Helsingør.
9.1946-4.1947: Hull repair and rebuilding with a new bow by Aarhus Flydedok A/S, Aarhus.
7.1947-8.1947: Work on main and auxiliary engines by Burmeister & Wain, Copenhagen.
21.3.1948: Trials after further work at Helsingør and Landskrona.
23.3.1955: Blown ashore off Plymouth.
26.3.1955: Refloated.
16.10.1968: Sold to Shipbreaking Industries Ltd.
20.10.1968: Breaking up began at Faslane.

Venus (2) inside and out. Compared with the photograph on page 130, she has a radar scanner fitted above her wheelhouse in addition to that on the foremast. *[Top: F.W. Hawks; others J. and M. Clarkson collection]*

Taken for Aarhus Flydedok A/S, these photographs show just how extensive was the work on the hull of *Venus* in late 1946 and early 1947. The forepart of the hull was completely dismantled and she was extensively replated. Postwar shortages of steel meant that most of the frames and plating was taken off, straightened, and put back on. *[Courtesy of Søren Thorsøe]*

This page: *Venus* (2) during an early post-war cruise at Funchal, Madeira (upper) and (lower) on 28th August 1965 by when her hull had been painted white and her funnels yellow with white bands. The old lady lost some of her dignity when dressed in white. *[Upper: F.W. Hawks collection; lower: J. and M. Clarkson]*

Opposite page top: the tragically short-lived *Vega* (2) of 1938. *[World Ship Photo Library collection]*
Opposite page middle: *Astrea [J. and M. Clarkson]*
Opposite page bottom: *Lyra. [Sammlung Siersdorfer 218/15A]*

VEGA (2) 1938-1945 Twin screw
7,287g 4,184n 424.6 x 58.3 x 28.5 feet.
Two 10-cyl. 2SCSA Sulzer-type oil engines by Cantieri Riuniti dell'Adriatico, Trieste driving twin screws; 2,270 NHP.
5.1938: Completed by Cantieri Riuniti dell'Adriatico, Trieste (Yard No. 1205) for Det Bergenske Dampskibsselskab, Bergen as VEGA.
3.1941: Requisitioned by Germany.
4.3.1945: Sunk by Russian aircraft.
By 30.6.1949: Salved. Midships section cut out and taken to Howaldtswerke where the engines were installed in the formerly steam-powered tankers KOLLGRIM (9,881/1941, Odd Bergs Tankrederi A/S (Odd Berg, manager), Oslo) and HAUKEFJELL (9,829/1941A/S Falkefjell (Olsen & Ugelstad, managers), Oslo).

ASTREA 1945-1967
3,190g 1,740n 313.2 x 44.1 x 24.0 feet.
7-cyl. 2SCSA oil engine by Friedrich Krupp Germaniawerft, Kiel.
10. 1939: Launched by Crichton-Vulcan A/B, Åbo (Yard No. 755) for Finska Ångfartygs A/B, Helsinki (Finland Line) as ASTREA but laid up owing to the war.
2.1944: Sold in a damaged condition to Stockholms Rederi A/B Svea, Stockholm. Secretly arranged that she would be sold on to Det Bergenske Dampskibsselskab, Bergen. Rebuilt by Finnboda Varv., Stockholm.
9. 1945: Commissioned by Det Bergenske Dampskibsselskab
11.1967: Sold to Pf Skipafelagid Føroyar, Torshavn, Faroes and re-named TJALDUR under the Norwegian flag.
18.7.1969: Engine breakdown.
28.8.1969: Sold to Metaalhandel en Sloopwerken H.P. Heuvelman N.V.
6.9.1969: Arrived under tow in the Nieuw Waterweg.
22.9.1969: Breaking up began at Krimpen a/d Ijssel, The Netherlands.

LYRA 1925-1954
1,474g 835n 241.5 x 34.6 x 15.4 feet.
T. 3-cyl. by A.G. 'Vulcan', Stettin; 148 NHP, 11 knots.
12.1911: Launched by A.G. 'Vulcan', Stettin (Yard No. 324) for Neue Dampfer-Kompagnie A.G., Stettin as PRINZ EITEL FRIEDRICH.
5.1912: Completed.
8.1914: Seized by Russia and taken to Reval.
8.1914: Became Imperial Russian Navy transport FERT.
6.1915: Became Russian minelayer URAL.
5.1920: Became depot ship for minesweepers.
12.1921: Returned to Neue Dampfer-Kompagnie A.G., Stettin.
1922: Renamed SCHLESIEN.
1923: Sold to Stettiner Dampfer-Kompagnie, Stettin.
1925: Acquired by Det Bergenske Dampskibsselskab, Bergen and renamed LYRA.
1940: Handed over to Nortraship and operated for the Allies.
1945: Returned to Det Bergenske Dampskibsselskab, Bergen.
1954: Sold to Sivert Bakke, Bergen and renamed NORA.
1954: Sold to Adel Abdul-Waha, Beirut, Lebanon, renamed LYRA and operated as a pilgrim ship.
9.7.1958: Wrecked at Tor harbour, Red Sea in position 28.12 north by 33.36 east whilst on a voyage from Jeddah to Suez with passengers, and became a total loss.

The second *Leda* was a powerful-looking, if not exactly pretty ship. In the middle photograph she is just about recognisable as the cruise ship *Albatros*. Bottom, she ends her days at Aliaga as *Star of Venice*. *[Top: J. and M. Clarkson; middle A. Molinari, author's collection; bottom: Selim San]*

LEDA (2) 1953-1976 Twin screw
6,670g 3,635n 436.8 x 57.2 x 26.2 feet.
Two sets of Parsons turbines by Wallsend Slipway Co. Ltd., Wallsend-on-Tyne, double-reduction geared to twin screws; 13,000 SHP.
4.1953: Completed by Swan, Hunter and Wigham Richardson Ltd., Newcastle-upon-Tyne (Yard No. 1823) for Det Bergenske Dampskibsselskab Bergen as LEDA.
9.1974: Laid up at Bergen.
1976: Sold to Stord Verft A/S for use as an accommodation ship.
1978: Sold to Kuwait Livestock Transport and Trading Co. Ltd., Kuwait.
1979: Renamed NAJLA (also rendered NALJA) and chartered for use as an accommodation ship for Lewis Offshore, Stornoway.
1981: Sold to Aspis Maritime S.A., Panama.
1981: Sold to Dolphin (Hellas) Shipping S.A., Panama and renamed ALBATROS under the Greek flag
1984: Completed much-interrupted conversion into a cruise ship.
1985: Renamed ALEGRO.
1988: Renamed BETSY ROSS.
1989: Sold to Beacon Maritime Seaways (National Transatlantic Lines of Greece S.A.), Piraeus and renamed AMALFI.
10.1989: Arrested at Venice for debt.
12.1990: Sold to Valgas Trading Ltd., Valetta (Stargas SpA, Mestre, Italy.)
1991: Renamed STAR OF VENICE under the Vanuatu flag.
1991: Damaged by fire; repaired at a Yugoslav yard.
1992: Became police accommodation ship at Genoa and later at Pianosa.
10.1992: Laid up at Venice.
1995: Sold to Star of Venice Navigation S.A., Panama (Pan Nautic S.A., Lugano).
2000: Became accommodation ship at Ravenna.
20.8.2001: Arrived at Aliaga to be broken up by Sok. Gemi Sokum Ltd.
5.9.2001: Breaking up began.

METEOR 1955-1970
2,856g 1,548n 296.7 x 45.1 x 15.1 feet.
Turbo-charged 9-cyl. 2SCSA oil engine by Burmeister & Wain, Copenhagen; 5,000 BHP.
1.1955: Completed by Aalborg Vaerft A/S, Aalborg (Yard No. 104) for Det Bergenske Dampskibsselskab Bergen as METEOR.
1960-1961: Converted into a full-time cruise ship by Aalborg Vaerft A/S.
1970: Transferred to Meteor Cruises A/S, Bergen.
22.5.1971: Severely damaged by fire whilst cruising near Vancouver.
10.1972: Sold to Epirotiki Steam Navigation Co. 'George Potamianos' of Piraeus, restored and renamed NEPTUNE (the Greek version, POSEIDON, appeared on her stern). She was initially renamed ZEPHIROS.
1985: Owners became Hellenic Co. for Mediterranean Cruises (Epirotiki Cruise Line, manager), Piraeus.
1996: Managers became Royal Olympic Cruises Ltd.
2.3.2002: Arrived at Aliaga to be broken up.

In contrast to the *Venus,* white paint seemed to suit the *Meteor.* Ironically, sale for service in the Mediterranean saw the sun deck forward abolished in favour of more accommodation. Apart from this, and a new funnel she was still recognisable as *Neptune* whilst awaiting her turn to be scrapped at Aliaga (bottom). *[F.W. Hawks; bottom: Selim San]*

JUPITER (2) 1966-1986 Twin-screw stern-loading ferry
9,499g 2,995n 464.7 x 66.5 x 21.4 feet.
Two 18-cyl. 4SCSA Pielstick-type oil engines by Ottensener Eisenwerke GmbH, Hamburg driving twin screws; 16,740 BHP, 22 knots.
6. 1966: Completed by Lübecker Flender-Werke, Lübeck (Yard No. 560) for joint ownership by Det Bergenske Dampskibsselskab, Bergen for whom she was registered as JUPITER and Fred. Olsen & Co., Oslo for whom she was registered as BLACK WATCH.
1982: Chartered to DFDS for several summer seasons.
1985: Chartered to Norway Line A/S, Bergen for summer seasons.
1986: Sold to Norway Line A/S, Bergen (Skaugen Marine A/S, Oslo, managers).
10.1990: Sold to Cadet Shipping Ltd., Panama (Marlines S.A. (Pan. Marangopoulos), Piraeus) and renamed CROWN M.
1992: Owners became Loryma Navigation Ltd., Limassol (Marlines S.A. (Pan. Marangopoulos), Piraeus).
About 26.9.1996: Laid up at Eleusis, reported as carrying the name BYBLOS.
1999: Owners became Philpot Shipping Ltd., Limassol (Marlines S.A. (Pan. Marangopoulos), Piraeus)
10.2002: Still in existence.

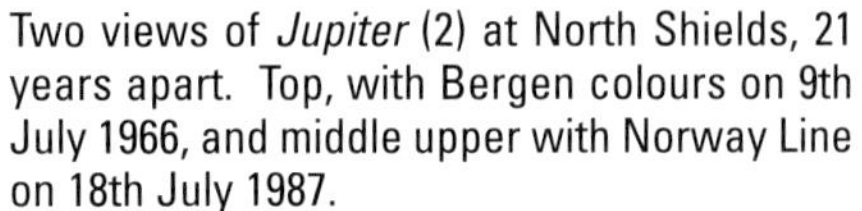
Two views of *Jupiter* (2) at North Shields, 21 years apart. Top, with Bergen colours on 9th July 1966, and middle upper with Norway Line on 18th July 1987.
[G.R. Scott; J. and M. Clarkson]

VENUS (3) 1968-1986 Twin-screw stern loading ferry
9,499g 2,995n 464.7 x 66.5 x 21.4 feet.
Two 18-cyl. 4SCSA Pielstick-type oil engines by Ottensener Eisenwerke GmbH, Hamburg driving twin screws; 16,740 BHP, 22.5 knots.
10.1966: Completed by Lübecker Flender-Werke, Lübeck (Yard No. 561) for Fred. Olsen & Co., Oslo as BLACK PRINCE.
1968: Det Bergenske Dampskibsselskab, Bergen bought a stake in the ship, which now had two registered names, VENUS for Bergenske and BLACK PRINCE for Fred. Olsen & Co.
28.5.1973: Badly damaged when she struck an underwater object at Trondheim.
1982: Chartered to DFDS for several summer seasons.
1986: Det Bergenske Dampskibsselskab share sold to Fred. Olsen & Co., Oslo.
1987: Converted into a 11,209 gross tons cruise ship, under the name BLACK PRINCE. Owners became Vinta Maritime Co. Inc., Manila (Blackfriars Shipping Ltd., London) (Fred. Olsen and Co., managers), and registered in Manila, Philippines.
1989: Owners became Black Prince Management Inc. (Black Prince Management Ltd., managers), Oslo, and registered in Oslo.
1994: Owners became P/R Ganger Rolf og Bonheur (Fred Olsen & Co., managers), Oslo, but now registered in Hvitsten, Norway.
1997: Owners became Partrederiet Fred. Olsen Shipping ANS (Fred Olsen & Co., managers), Oslo.
1999: Owners became P/R Ganger Rolf SAS og Bonheur ASA (Red Band A/S, managers), Oslo.
2002: Registered in Nassau, Bahamas.
10.2002: Still in service.

Venus (middle lower) in original condition and (bottom) as *Black Prince* at Warnemunde on 6th June 2001.
[J. and M. Clarkson; Wolfgang Kramer]

EVERY PICTURE TELLS A STORY

We had closed the door on further photographs of elderly Spaniards until this fascinating shot turned up. It leaves no doubt about the joys of carrying a cargo of coke, so light that it more than fills her wells. Note how the derricks are submerged, and how the companionway to the forecastle has been protected with wood. There is some sort of walkway laid over the after holds, presumably to give access to the poop.

The steamer *Uribitarte* was built at Burntisland in 1922 for owners in Bilbao, her yard number 114 being somewhat misleading, as the newly-established builders started counting at 100. In 1933 she was sold to Antonio Menchaca, also of Bilbao, and was in his ownership when this shot was taken over 30 years later. However, between 1936 and 1938, the Spanish Nationalist Government had placed her under the Italian flag as *Cosenza*. She then returned to Menchaca's ownership, completing her career with his company in 1972 when the 50-year-old veteran was broken up at Bilbao. *[Fotoflite incorporating Skyfotos]*

PHOTOGRAPHER IN FOCUS
WILLIAM LIVERMORE OF SYDNEY

Ian Farquhar

A century ago, the port of Sydney, Australia was a significant shipping terminus for the main line trades from United Kingdom and Europe. By this time much larger, more efficient vessels had replaced many of the first generation steamers. It was also a port of call for regular liner services from the Far East and North America.

A photographer who provided an important record of Sydney shipping between 1895 and 1925 was William Livermore. Although a portrait and general photographer, Livermore took a keen interest in maritime photography, initially using a whole plate camera (8 x 6 inches) and later a half plate model. In those days the volume shipping routes lay between Britain and her colonies. In this respect Livermore's contribution to maritime history is complimented by F.C. Gould and Son of Gravesend and D.A. de Maus in Port Chalmers. The material still extant by these three makes up the bulk of the photographic coverage of sailing ships and steamers in the England/Australia and New Zealand services over a century ago.

William Livermore was born in London and his family migrated to New Zealand in 1861. There were important gold discoveries in New Zealand in the 1860s and perhaps the lure of gold took him to Australia some years later. He married in Bathurst in 1874 and subsequently made a career as a photographer, setting up his first studio in 1887 and from 1898 generally trading under the name of the Star Photo Company. He moved from the Sydney suburb of Newton to a Pitt Street office in 1903. This location was very close to the port and it was from this time that he took most of his shipping material. Although the main business of the Star Photo Company was the production of postcard scenes of Sydney and the surrounding countryside, Livermore produced contact prints of the 8 x 6 plates for sale to personnel on the ships and for passengers who had travelled on them. In later years with the half plate camera he invariably masked the plates to postcard size (or 'cabinet' size as he described them). The whole plate prints were sold for nine pence each and the stationery of the company recorded that 'We make shipping views a speciality'. The Star Photo Company operated from several Sydney locations between 1898 and 1928. William Livermore died on 5th March 1925 and in the 1930s his glass plate shipping collection was acquired by one of Australia's most prolific collectors of shipping material, Captain Walter F. Lee (1885-1956) of Adelaide. With both his paternal and maternal grandfathers and his father being master mariners, Walter Lee went to sea in sailing ships, serving his apprenticeship in the barque *Bankfields*. He joined Coast Steamships of Adelaide in 1909 and transferred to The Adelaide Steamship Company in 1928, remaining with that company until his retirement in 1950. Whilst many photographic collectors just accumulate material, Walter Lee endeavoured to secure a photographic record of every ship a company owned and he supplied illustrations to such well known writers as Alan Villiers, Basil Lubbock and Dickson Gregory. In order that the steamship collection passed to someone younger with a similar interest it was acquired by the writer in 1955. The Lee family sold all the plates of sailing ships to the Allen Knight Museum of Monterey, California after Lee's death in 1956. These included quite a number taken by William Livermore. The Allen Knight Museum now forms part of the Monterey Maritime Museum and the Lee Collection of some 3,400 sailing ships is maintained as a separate collection within the Allen Knight section of the museum.

The following prints taken from Livermore glass whole plates provide some fine examples of his maritime photography in the first few years of the twentieth century.

AIRLIE
William Doxford and Sons, Sunderland; 1884, 2,337gt, 314 feet
C. 2-cyl. by Hawks, Crawshay and Company, Newcastle-upon-Tyne; 308 NHP
Built for the Eastern and Australian Steamship Company service between Singapore, Hong Kong and Foochow and eastern Australian ports, *Airlie* sailed from Sunderland for Singapore on 19th July 1884. She and her sister ship *Guthrie* were smart-looking iron steamers with a clipper bow under which was affixed the figurehead of a woman. They had accommodation for 60 passengers and maintained a service speed of 11/12 knots. Apart from spending nine days on a reef at Chatham Island, 200 miles north of Cooktown, Queensland in 1900, *Airlie* had a very reliable twenty years with E and A. In 1904 she was sold to Burns Philp and Company of Sydney and employed in that company's service to Singapore via ports in Papua New Guinea and the Dutch East Indies. The photograph shows the *Airlie* with the distinctive Burns Philp funnel colours. *Airlie* was replaced by the *Mataram* in 1909 and she made one further voyage from Sydney to Hong Kong in 1910. From there she was sold to Chinese shipbreakers.

EMPIRE (above)
William Beardmore and Co., Glasgow; 1902, 4,496 gt, 386 feet
T. 3-cyl. by William Beardmore and Co., Glasgow; 613 NHP
In immaculate condition, the two-year-old E and A liner *Empire* sails down Sydney harbour on 2nd July 1904. The Eastern and Australian Steamship Company had commenced its service from Singapore to Australia through the Torres Strait in 1873 and *Empire* was the fourteenth ship specially built for the service. By the time she began running, the range of eastern ports included Manila, Hong Kong, Foochow, Shanghai, Moji, Kobe and Yokohama. She was the last of the fleet to be built with a clipper bow. With accommodation for 70 passengers in first class and 50 in second class, she also had provision for the carriage of many coolies. After nearly 18 years' service her machinery was becoming increasingly more expensive to operate and she was sold in 1920 to the Compagnie Generale Transatlantique of Paris and became the *Volubilis* under the French flag. She was sold to Dutch shipbreakers in March 1932.

KYARRA (below)
William Denny and Brothers, Dumbarton; 1903, 6,953gt, 416 feet
T. 8-cyl. by William Denny and Brothers, Dumbarton; 770 NHP
The Australasian United Steam Navigation Company sisters *Kyarra* (shown here in June 1904) and *Kanowna* were the largest Australian interstate passenger ships of their time. They were employed on monthly round voyages between Sydney, Melbourne, Adelaide and Fremantle. Accommodation was provided for 125 passengers in first class, 136 second class and 250 third class. From 1912 to 1914 *Kyarra* ran on the tourist route from Melbourne to Queensland calling at Sydney, Brisbane, Rockhampton, Mackay, Bowen, Townsville and Cairns. Requisitioned during the First World War, she was fitted out as a hospital ship with a 1,640-bed capacity. She later became an armed transport and was torpedoed and sunk by UB 57 in the English Channel on 25th May 1918, sinking in sixteen minutes with the loss of six lives.

ROME (above)
Caird and Company, Greenock; 1881, 5,013gt, 430 feet (1881), 5,545gt, 449 (1891)
C. 4-cyl. inverted tandem (1881), T. 4-cyl. both by Caird and Company, Greenock, 775 NHP (1891)
The first of the four-masted, barque-rigged, two-funnelled P&O liners in the London/Australia service was the iron hulled *Rome* built in 1881. Accommodation was provided for 187 passengers in first class and 146 passengers in second class. On her maiden voyage *Rome* was the first P&O liner to sail from Tilbury (4th October 1881) with the traditional call at Southampton being abandoned. Apart from steering difficulties and a grounding in 1887, she had ten successful years in the Australian trade, before undergoing a major refit. New engines were fitted by Caird, her bow section was replaced which saw *Rome* lengthened by 19 feet. An unfortunate fire in the shipyard also required much of the passenger accommodation to be rebuilt. All the yards were removed and the illustration shows the vessel in post-1891 rig. In 1903 she left the Australian service and was refitted by P&O as the cruise liner *Vectis* doing short sea cruises to the Baltic, Mediterranean and Atlantic Islands. Sold to the French Government in 1912, she was scrapped in Italy a year later.

BRITANNIA (below)
Caird and Company, Greenock; 1887, 6,525gt, 466 feet
T. 3-cyl. by Caird and Company, Greenock, 849 NHP
Photographed in June 1904, the P&O liner *Britannia* was designed for the company's Australian service and made her maiden voyage from Tilbury on 4th November 1887. Her triple expansion steam engines could provide a speed of 16.5 knots and on her maiden voyage she delivered the mail from Brindisi to Adelaide in a record 23 days 10 hours. With accommodation for 230 passengers in first class and 156 in second class, she was a sister ship to *Victoria, Oceana* and *Arcadia.* With their four pole masts and two thin funnels, they were distinctive vessels for their day. From 1887 to 1909 she ran to Australia apart from occasional voyages on the Indian and Far Eastern services and periods between 1894-97 as an Indian troopship. *Britannia* made her last sailing for Australia in August 1908 and the following year she was sold to Italian shipbreakers, arriving at Genoa for demolition on 22nd August 1909.

INDIA (above)
Caird and Company, Greenock; 1896, 9,911gt, 500 feet
T. 4-cyl. by Caird and Company, Greenock; 1,321 NHP
First of a new class of two-funnelled passenger vessels for the P&O Indian or Australian services, *India* was initially employed on the run to Bombay. She made her first voyage from London to Australia on 28th January 1898. With accommodation for 317 passengers in first class and 152 in second class, *India* and *China* spent most of their time on the Australian service while the other sisters, *Egypt, Arabia* and *Persia,* served the route to India. The ships had been built to meet Admiralty specifications so they could be employed as troopships or armed merchant cruisers. *India* proved a popular vessel and made her last Australian run in 1911. When the First World War broke out, she was converted to an Armed Merchant Cruiser. On 8th August 1915 she was torpedoed and sunk by *U 22* off Helligvaer, close to Bodo in Norway with the loss of 160 lives.

ORUBA (below)
Naval Construction and Armaments Co. Ltd., Barrow-in-Furness; 1889, 5,857gt, 430 feet
T. 3-cyl. by Naval Construction and Armaments Co. Ltd., Barrow-in-Furness; 764NHP
With the crew stowing the port anchor and the lookout man in the crow's nest, the *Oruba* sails down Sydney harbour flying the Royal Mail pennant and the Orient Line house flag. Although built for the South American service of the Pacific Steam Navigation Company, *Oruba* made her maiden voyage to Australia in July 1890. She was transferred to the Orient-Royal Mail Line service in 1906 following the purchase of the four Pacific Steam vessels *(Oroya, Orotava, Oruba* and *Ortona)* by the Royal Mail Steam Packet Company. The arrangement between the two companies did not work well and in 1909 they split with Royal Mail withdrawing the four ships although *Oruba* had made her last voyage in 1908. She then ran on the West Indies service until 1914 when she was acquired by the Admiralty and converted into the dummy battleship HMS *Orion* stationed at Mudros in the Aegean Sea. She was later scuttled at Mudros.

DAMASCUS (above)
Robert Napier and Sons, Glasgow; 1887, 3,726 gt, 362 feet
T. 3-cyl. by Robert. Napier and Sons, Glasgow; 409 NHP
The first steel vessel built for the Aberdeen Line of Geo. Thompson and Company was the *Damascus*. She left London on her maiden voyage to Adelaide, Melbourne and Sydney via Cape Town on 17th January 1888 and took her last sailing in this service on 18th February 1908. The attractive lines of the Aberdeen Line vessels with their three masts, clipper bows, dark green hulls and yellow funnels made them quite distinctive and they were popular ships in which to travel. Their owners also kept the vessels in immaculate condition. *Damascus* took her name from one of the earlier Aberdeen Line sailing ships of 1857. She was sold to N.G. Pittaluga of Genoa in 1909 and was broken up in that port in 1910.

SOPHOCLES (below)
Harland and Wolff, Belfast; 1883, 4,673gt, 440 feet
C. 4-cyl., 500 NHP (1883), Q. 4-cyl., 595 NHP (1894) both by Harland and Wolff.
Sophocles was one of the more attractive steamers of the nineteenth century. Originally built for the White Star Line as *Ionic,* she and her sister *Doric* were the first steel vessels in the White Star fleet. Each ship had accommodation for 70 passengers and was fitted out for the carriage of refrigerated cargo. In 1894 *Ionic* had an extensive refit with the compound engine being replaced with quadruple expansion machinery. She was purchased in 1900 by the Aberdeen Line as a replacement for the wrecked *Thermopylae. Ionic* had been employed on the New Zealand trade so the rename to *Sophocles* saw her operating on much the same ocean route from London, via Cape Town but terminating in Sydney. She left on her first Aberdeen Line sailing on 23rd October 1900 and her last sailing was six years later. She was broken up at Morecambe in 1908.

SUEVIC (above)
Harland and Wolff Ltd., Belfast, 1900, 12,531gt, 550 feet
Q. 6-cyl. by Harland and Wolff Ltd., Belfast; 641 NHP
Slipping along down Sydney Harbour, the *Suevic* had the appearance of a large, voracious cargo carrier. Her refrigerated cargo spaces could carry the equivalent of 112,000 (27 kg) frozen lambs. She was the last in a series of five large refrigerated cargo ships built by White Star Line for employment in the Australian trade. She sailed on her maiden voyage from Liverpool to Albany, Adelaide, Melbourne and Sydney via Cape Town on 23rd March 1901. When she stranded in fog on Stag Rock, near the Lizard on 17th March 1907, her subsequent salvage drew worldwide attention. The after portion of the ship was salved and towed to Southampton. There it was fitted to a new bow section hastily built at Belfast. *Suevic* was back in service by January 1908. Employed as a troop transport during the First World War, she resumed in the Australian trade from 1920. In 1928 she was sold to Norwegian whaling interests and converted to the factory ship *Skytteren.* Swedish neutrality saw her interned at Gothenburg in April 1940. When attempting to reach the safety of a British port, she was scuttled by her own crew near Maseskjaer, Sweden on 1st April 1942 when German naval vessels were about to seize her (see *Record* 5, pages 46-47).

CHINGTU (below)
Scott and Company, Greenock; 1886, 2,268 gt, 315 feet
T. 3-cyl. by Scott and Company, Greenock; 266 NHP
Chingtu burning the Newcastle (N.S.W.) coal as she steams out of Sydney in August 1905. One of four sister ships *(Changsha, Taiyuan, Tsinan* and *Chingtu)* which were built for the China Navigation Company's Australian service, *Chingtu* made her maiden voyage south from Hong Kong on 11th January 1887. The vessels operated a regular service from Hong Kong to Townsville, Brisbane, Sydney and Melbourne via Thursday Island with calls at Newcastle for bunkers. In later years the operating costs of the vessels were too expensive and *Chingtu* was sold to a Wallem and Company subsidiary in 1909 being renamed *Chingtuan.* In 1910 she was under the Norwegian flag as the *Chingtufu* and in 1914 she went to the Russian Volunteer Fleet of Vladivostok and was renamed *Yana.* Sold to Japanese owners in 1923 she was wrecked as the *Toyokuni Maru* on 2nd April 1929 at Cape Erino, near Hakodate, Hokkaido, Japan.

STAR OF NEW ZEALAND (above)
Workman, Clark and Co. Ltd., Belfast; 1895, 4,840gt, 394 feet
T. 3-cyl. by Workman, Clark and Co. Ltd., Belfast; 457 NHP
Built for The Star Line Limited of James P. Corry and Company of Belfast, the *Star of New Zealand* was fitted out with refrigerated space and was operated on the Tyser Line berth in the New Zealand and Australian trades. She is shown here lying at Tyser's Wharf in Sydney. Vessels loaded out from both the United Kingdom and the East Coast of North America and then invariably loaded frozen meat in New Zealand under contracts first gained by Tyser and Company in 1886. As more modern tonnage was introduced into the Australasian services, *Star of New Zealand* was chartered out to other lines seeking refrigerated tonnage. She ran aground off Molene, near Brest on 28th November 1915 while on passage from Montevideo to Havre with a full cargo of frozen meat. She was abandoned on 4th December as a total loss.

MARERE (below)
Workman, Clark and Co. Ltd., Belfast; 1902, 6,443gt, 450 feet
T. 6-cyl. by Workman, Clark and Co. Ltd., Belfast; 583 NHP
The refrigerated cargo liner *Marere* was specially built for the Tyser Line service from London to Australia. Most of the vessels in the service then crossed over to New Zealand to load back refrigerated cargo and wool. Tyser Line also chartered ships of the James P. Corry Star Line, and worked together with Royden Line in a service from North America to Australia. The company was the catalyst in 1914 in bringing all three lines together with Wm. Milburn's Anglo Australasian Steam Navigation Company to form the Commonwealth and Dominion Line Ltd. All the vessels were intended to be given names beginning with *Port* and *Marere* was the only vessel of the combined company that was not renamed. Following the outbreak of war, she had been fitted out as Australian transport *A21* to carry 10 officers, 100 other ranks and 465 horses, and was a unit of the first large convoy to leave Australian waters in November 1914. She was shelled and sunk by the German submarine *U 35* 236 miles from Malta on 18th January 1916.

PORT PHILLIP (above)
Hawthorn, Leslie and Co. Ltd., Newcastle-upon-Tyne; 1906, 4,060gt, 380 feet
T. 3-cyl. by Hawthorn Leslie and Co. Ltd., Newcastle-upon-Tyne; 442 NHP
In immaculate condition and dressed for a Sydney regatta day, *Port Phillip* lies anchored in Sydney harbour in January 1908. Owned by William Milburn and Co. of London, *Port Phillip* ran under the auspices of The Anglo-Australasian Steam Navigation Company, a subsidiary company which had operated regular sailings between London, Adelaide, Melbourne, Sydney and Newcastle from 1883. The ships all had Port names and the line was a major carrier of Australian wool. In 1914 *Port Phillip* was one of nine Milburn ships that transferred to the Commonwealth and Dominion Line Ltd. when it was formed. On 16th October 1918 *Port Phillip* sank in the Ambrose Channel, New York, following a collision with USS *Proteus*.

ROSETTA MARU (below)
Harland and Wolff, Belfast; 1880, 3,876gt, 384 feet
C. 2-cyl. by J. Howden and Co., Glasgow; 570 NHP
After several trial voyages, Nippon Yusen Kaisha (NYK) of Tokyo commenced a regular passenger, mail and cargo service to Australia in 1896. Most of the vessels employed were built in British shipyards specifically for the company. At that time all the masters were British and it was not until 1907 that Japanese masters were experienced enough to take over command. To replace the two-year-old *Futami Maru* which was wrecked in August 1900 on Mindoro Island in the Philippines, the *Rosetta Maru* was brought into the service from December 1900/November 1901. Previously P&O's *Rosetta* between 1880 and 1900, NYK resold *Rosetta Maru* immediately after her Australian voyages. She then remained under the ownership of other Japanese companies until scrapped in 1907. Apart from the name change the photograph shows her distinctive lines as a P&O vessel.

GERA (above)
Fairfield Shipbuilding and Engineering Co. Ltd., Glasgow; 1890, 5,005gt, 413 feet
T. 3-cyl. by Fairfield Shipbuilding and Engineering Co. Ltd., Glasgow; 506 NHP
Norddeutscher Lloyd of Bremen commenced a monthly liner service from Bremerhaven to Adelaide, Melbourne and Sydney in 1886 with calls at Antwerp, Southampton, Genoa, Port Said and Suez. *Gera,* pictured in 1904, was built in 1890 but did not make her maiden voyage to Australia until November 1893. Thereafter, she and her sisters, *Darmstadt, Karlsruhe, Stuttgart, Oldenburg* and *Weimar,* were regulars on the route. The vessels had accommodation for 49 passengers in first class, 38 in second class and up to 1,900 in steerage as the service specifically targeted migrant traffic. *Gera* made her last Australian voyage in 1906 and two years later she was sold to Lloyd del Pacifico of Savona for that company's service from Italy to Chile. She was renamed *Valparaiso* and was lost off Marsa Susa, Libya on 14th October 1917 after being torpedoed by *UB 48.*

STASSFURT (opposite lower)
Blohm and Voss, Hamburg; 1891, 3,231gt, 341 feet
T. 3-cyl. by Blohm and Voss, Hamburg; 329 NHP
The Deutsch-Australische Dampfschiff-ahrts Gesellschaft (The German-Australian Steamship Company) was established by Hamburg merchants in 1888 as they felt they were being left out of the German-Australian trade by the domination of the Norddeutscher Lloyd from Bremen. The first sailing from Hamburg, Amsterdam and Antwerp for Adelaide, Melbourne and Sydney commenced 24th July 1889 and within a few years the line was also calling at Cape Town en route and returning via ports in the Dutch East Indies. Norddeutscher Lloyd was an important migrant carrier while The German-Australian Steamship Company concentrated almost solely on cargo. The ships were sparsely run and the line was often called the German Austerity Line! *Stassfurt* was built for the service in 1891 and she was typical of the German Australian Line cargo ships of that period. She was sold to the Deutsche Levante Linie of Hamburg in 1906 and renamed *Chios*. She foundered in heavy weather on 21st December 1911 in the Bay of Biscay on passage from the Tees to Oran.

MARIPOSA (top)
William Cramp and Sons, Philadelphia; 1883, 3,158gt, 314 feet
C. 3-cyl. by William Cramp and Sons, Philadelphia; 443 NHP
The Oceanic Steamship Company, owned by the Spreckels family of San Francisco, introduced a subsidised mail and passenger service from San Francisco to Honolulu, Auckland and Sydney in 1885 with the *Mariposa* leaving San Francisco on her first voyage on 20th December. With her sister ship *Alameda,* she remained in the trade until replaced by larger vessels in 1901. In 1902 she commenced running in the shorter San Francisco/Tahiti service and continued between the two ports until 1912. She was then sold to Alaska Steamship Company and ended her days when she was wrecked on Straits Island Reef, five miles west from Wrangell, Alaska on 18th November 1917.

SONOMA (above)
William Cramp and Sons Company, Philadelphia; 1900, 6,523gt, 400 feet
T. 6-cyl. by William Cramp and Sons Company, Philadelphia; 1,036 NHP
The Oceanic Steamship Company replaced the smaller *Mariposa* and *Alameda* on the San Francisco/Sydney service in 1901 with three new larger vessels - *Sierra, Sonoma* and *Ventura.* Each ship had accommodation for 238 passengers in first class, 80 second class and 84 in steerage. In 1907 the U.S. Government removed the mail subsidy and it was not until 1912 that the *Sonoma* and *Ventura* returned to the service. By this time *Sonoma* was burning oil instead of coal and she had one large funnel instead of the two funnels shown in this earlier photograph. Oceanic Steamship Company was sold to Matson Line in 1926 and *Sonoma* continued on the run until 1932 when Matson introduced the liners *Mariposa* and *Monterey.* Sold to Japanese ship breakers in 1932, she was renamed *Sonoma Maru* for the delivery voyage to Osaka.

THE IRON LADIES Part 1

John Harrison

'Most of the specialised ore carriers covered by the study were on long term charter to BISC (Ore) Ltd. on terms designed to provide a reasonable return on the capital outlay and this had easily been the most profitable sector of the (shipping) industry.'

Thus stated the Government's Committee of Inquiry into Shipping, the Rochdale Report, published in 1970. This comment related to a series of 73 ore carriers built for long term charter to the British Iron and Steel Corporation (BISC) (Ore), starting with the *Ormsary* launched by Lady Lithgow at Lithgow's yard on the Clyde on 26rd August 1952 and ending with the *Victore* completed by Austin and Pickersgill in December 1963. These articles look at this series of ships and trace their careers.

A revolutionary concept

Before the Second World War and immediately afterwards, it was the usual practice to carry iron ore in general cargo vessels which made transportation costs comparatively expensive. To reduce these costs for the ore needed for rebuilding post war British industry, the then recently formed British Iron and Steel Corporation commissioned a series of purpose-built ore carriers for long term charter to the Corporation. These ships were of what was considered at the outset of the project to be revolutionary design, though most of the innovatory features are now the norm for bulk carriers and indeed other types of ship. The engines and accommodation were placed aft, though some ships did have their bridges amidships. Large hatch openings provided access to box tanks with wing tanks for water ballast, capable of taking ballast equal to approximately two thirds of the ship's deadweight to facilitate handling when running light. No cargo handling gear was fitted, loading and unloading being carried out by facilities ashore.

The introduction of these ships considerably reduced transportation costs for BISC when compared with the costs for the general cargo tramps that were previously used. Furthermore, having ships directly under their control was a logistically much simpler process than the previous practice of chartering in ships, either for individual voyages or for short periods. As indicated by the Rochdale Report, however, such charters were also profitable for the companies owning the ships. The purchase of the ships represented a fixed cost to their owners, normally financed by a loan or overdraft. As the charters continued these loans were gradually paid off and the rate of return increased. It should be noted that the charter agreements included escalation clauses to allow for inflation. These were based on crew wages as the Corporation thought these would be the best indicator of the rate of inflation over charter periods. In fact crewing cost was the cost that rose fastest over the period. Thus, by the end of the charter periods, they proved to be very remunerative.

Charter periods were normally 10 or 15 years, but two ships, the *Gerore* and the *Welsh Herald,* had charter periods of 13 years and the *Filefjell* had a charter period of only five years. The ships fell into three size categories and the *Filefjell* was the first of the largest type. The short length of the charter period was an indication that BISC were unwilling to commit themselves to a longer period for what was at that time considered a very large ship. The *Morar,* which was an experimental gas turbine vessel, proved to be unreliable and this resulted in the early termination of her charter by mutual agreement after nine years.

Ormsary, first of the ore carriers completed for charter to the British Iron and Steel Corporation. *[Fotoflite incorporating Skyfotos]*

Partnership companies in which BISC had a 49% stake

Title	Other participants
St. Denis Shipping Co. Ltd.	Wm. Cory and Son Ltd.
Ore Carriers Ltd.	Houlder Bros. and Co. Ltd.
Bamburgh Shipping Co. Ltd.	W.A. Souter and Co. Ltd.
St. Andrews Shipping Co. Ltd.	J. and J. Denholm Ltd
North Yorkshire Shipping Co. Ltd.	Bolton Steam Shipping Co. Ltd. and Smith's Dock Ltd.
Bishopgate Shipping Co. Ltd.	Silver Line Ltd., Sir J. Laing and Sons Ltd., and Thompsons Ltd.
Vallum Shipping Co. Ltd.	Common Bros. Ltd. and Jardine Matheson Ltd.

Although most of the ships were directly chartered from shipowners, in a number of cases they were chartered from owning companies in which BISC had a 49% stake, the other parties having a 51% stake. The main reason for these partnership arrangements was to encourage ship owners reluctant to take part in building ships of what were considered at that time unconventional design. The partnership companies are listed above.

Most of the ships were owned by British shipping companies. Twelve were under the Norwegian flag and the *Philippe LD* owned by Louis Dreyfus et Compagnie flew the French flag. The *Orecrest* of Ivanovic was registered in Nassau, Bahamas. The Furness Withy ships, *Edenmore* and *Sagamore,* were originally to have been registered in Bermuda, but following an increase in the investment allowance to 40% they were registered in Britain. The *Victore* was similarly also to have been registered in Bermuda, but was finally registered under the British flag.

As a corollary of the chartering programme, it was decided to concentrate iron ore imports on a limited number of United Kingdom ports. This enabled specialist cargo handling facilities for iron ore to be installed to reduce costs further. The efficiencies that resulted from these ships and related improvements in cargo handling facilities can be illustrated by the *Gleddoch,* the second ship in the series to be completed. On Monday 13th July 1953 she arrived at Port Talbot with a cargo of iron ore from Narvik. Discharging took less than nine hours, an average hourly discharge rate of almost 1,000 tons. This performance was at that time believed to be a record rate of discharge for any port in the United Kingdom. It was estimated that the *Gleddoch* and her sistership, the *Ormsary,* the first two of the ore carriers, took half the time to load compared with a conventional single deck cargo ship.

Types of ore carrier

The ships were designed to use a limited number of ports both in Britain and abroad. Ore was primarily imported from Scandinavia, Spain, West and North Africa, Eastern Canada and Brazil. The sizes of the ships were constrained by the restrictions of the ports used. As has been mentioned, the ships fell into three size ranges.

The smaller class was known as the Port Talbot type as their dimensions were the maximum which fitted the locks that at that time controlled the entrance to Port Talbot docks; 427 feet overall length, 57 feet beam and 24 feet draught (130 metres x 17.4 metres x 7.3 metres). These dimensions also meant the ships were a suitable size to use the Manchester Ship Canal to reach Irlam Steelworks and to enter the port of Workington. The deadweight of these ships was around 9,500 tons. There were 24 ships in this class.

The second class of ships had dimensions of 69 feet (21 metres) beam and a draught of 28 feet (8.5 metres). The overall length of these vessels was between 505 feet and 525 feet (154 to 160 metres) - the maximum length of vessel was gradually increased. The beam of 69 feet was determined by the maximum reach of the grabs at some of the loading and discharging ports. The constraints for the other dimensions were the locks at the entrances to Newport and Birkenhead Docks and the approaches to the ore berths on the Tees and at Rothbury Dock, Glasgow. As far as I am aware, this class of ship has not got a name, so for the purposes of this article I will refer to them as the intermediate class. There were 44 ships in this class with a deadweight of around 15,000 tons.

The series was completed by a third group of ships, the *Cape Howe, Filefjell, Gothland, Victore* and *Welsh Herald.* These had a length of approximately 600 feet, a beam of 80 feet and a draft of 32 feet (183 metres x 24 metres x 9.75 metres). Deadweight tonnages of these ships ranged from just over 25,000 tons to just under 32,000 tones. For the purpose of this article I will refer to this class as the larger type.

Furness Withy's *Edenmore* was originally to have been registered in Bermuda where the owners had substantial interests. *[Roy Fenton collection]*

Building

All the non-British ships were built in Continental yards. With the exception of the *La Colina* which, like her French sister ship, was built by Chantiers Reunis Loire-Normandie GD, Quevilly, the British-owned ships were built in British yards. British shipbuilding was still in its heyday.

At the time of their building the larger classes of vessel were considered very large cargo ships. Thus quite a few records were broken in building these ships. The *Joya McCance* being one frame larger than her sister ship, the *Mabel Warwick,* was the largest ship built by William Gray at Hartlepool. She was one of the last ships to be built before the closure of this yard. These two ships also had the distinction of being among the first British ships to have rounded gunwales at the upper deck. The *Cape Howe* was at the time of her building the largest ship built by Lithgows, a record that subsequently fell to the *Gothland.* The *Mesna* was when completed the largest ship built by Scheeps. de Biesbosch, Dordrecht. At Austin and Pickersgill, Sunderland, the *Iron Barque* was the largest ship built by the yard, a record that subsequently fell to the *Longstone,* and then to the *Victore* and the *Welsh Herald.* It should be noted that the *Needles* had earlier been the last ship to be completed by that company's East Yard.

Being of relatively simple construction, many of these ore carriers were built comparatively quickly. For instance, the *Craigallian* took 30 weeks to build from laying down to trials. Similarly the *Finnamore Meadow* was built by Austin and Pickersgills in five months and this feat was marked by the making of a BBC television documentary about her construction.

The designers of the Port Talbot ships had to attempt to fit the maximum cargo capacity into the tight dimensions that the Port Talbot docks allowed. On the *La Colina* and *Philippe LD,* by using a very full hull form and lightweight machinery, a deadweight tonnage of 9,700 tons was obtained. This was surpassed by the *Arabella, Essex, Farland* and *Gerland* which were built to a common design by a Norwegian firm of naval architects and had a deadweight of over 10,000 tons. Originally the design was just for one ship, the *Essex,* but she was so successful that orders were placed for the other three ships by their respective Norwegian owners.

To be continued.

FLEET LIST Part 1

This is a list of the 73 ships grouped by owning or managing companies. The letters PT after a ship's name indicate a ship of the Port Talbot type. The letter L indicates a ship of the largest type. Ships with no letters after their name are of the intermediate type. Tonnages and dimensions given are normally those quoted for the ship when she first appears in 'Lloyd's Register'. The dimensions given are length overall x extreme breadth x draft summer in feet and inches.

BRITISH FLAG

BOLTON STEAM SHIPPING CO. LTD.
North Yorkshire Shipping Co. Ltd. (Bolton Steam Shipping Co. Ltd., managers), London

REDCAR 1955-1971

O.N. 187304 10,746g 5,437n 15,244d 505'0" x 69'1" x 28'11"
4-cyl. 2SCSA Doxford-type oil engine by Hawthorn Leslie (Engineering) Ltd., Newcastle-upon-Tyne; 670 x 2,320, 4,450 BHP, 11.5 knots.
31.10.1955: Launched by Smith's Dock Co. Ltd., Middlesbrough (Yard No. 1238) for the North Yorkshire Shipping Co. Ltd. (Bolton Steam Shipping Co. Ltd., managers), London as REDCAR.
3.1956: Completed.
1969: Owners became Bolton Steam Shipping Co. Ltd., London
1971: Sold to St. Andrews Shipping Co. Ltd. (J. and J. Denholm (Management) Ltd., managers), Glasgow and renamed DUNBLANE.
1973: Sold to Compania Ady SA, Panama (Leonidas N. Pothas, Piraeus, Greece) and renamed ADY under the Greek flag.
7.1975: Laid up at Piraeus.
13.12.1978: Arrived at La Spezia for demolition by Terrestre Marittima SpA.

All four ships of the North Yorkshire Shipping Co. Ltd. were named after towns or villages in the North Riding of Yorkshire. This is *Redcar.* *[World Ship Photo Library]*

Ribblehead, assisted by Lamey tugs, makes her way through the Birkenhead dock system to discharge in Bidston Dock. *[Ken Cunnington]*

RIBBLEHEAD 1955-1972
O.N. 187310 10,741g 5,513n 15,300d 505'1" x 69'0" x 28'11½"
4-cyl. 2SCSA Doxford-type oil engine by David Rowan and Co. Ltd., Glasgow; 670 x 2,320, 4,450 BHP, 11.5 knots.
7.4.1957: Launched by Lithgows Ltd., Port Glasgow (Yard No. 1112) for the North Yorkshire Shipping Co. Ltd. (Bolton Steam Shipping Co. Ltd., managers), London as RIBBLEHEAD.
6.1957: Completed.
1969: Owners became Bolton Steam Shipping Co. Ltd., London.
1972: Sold to Antiklia Compania Naviera SA, Panama (Leonidas N. Pothas, Piraeus, Greece) and renamed ANTIKLIA under the Greek flag.
1978: Sold to Aramis Navigation Co. Ltd., Limassol, Cyprus (E. Pothitos, E. Koutsofios and others, Piraeus, Greece) and renamed EVPO ARAMIS.
2.5.1979: Ran aground near Jeddah and suffered bottom damage.
4.5.1979: Refloated.
8.4.1982: Arrived at Bombay for demolition by Ghaziram Gokul Chand and Co.
11.1982: Work commenced.

RIEVAULX 1957-1973
O.N. 187312 10,974g 5,514n 15,400d 505'0" x 69'1" x 28'11"
4-cyl. 2SCSA Doxford-type oil engine by Hawthorn Leslie (Engineering) Ltd., Newcastle-upon-Tyne; 670 x 2,320, 4,450 BHP, 11.5 knots.
27.8.1957: Launched by Smith's Dock Co. Ltd., Middlesbrough (Yard No. 1249) for the North Yorkshire Shipping Co. Ltd. (Bolton Steam Shipping Co. Ltd., managers), London as RIEVAULX.
6.1958: Completed.
1969: Owners became Bolton Steam Shipping Co. Ltd., London.
1973: Sold to Silver Lake Shipping Co. SA, Panama (Stavros A. Daifas, Piraeus, Greece) for £195,000 and renamed SILVER LAKE under the Greek flag.
1973: Sold to Kimolos Shipping Co. SA (Armada Marine SA (A.S. Manes), Piraeus, Greece) and renamed NEMA under the Greek flag.
16.6.1974: Collided with the NATCREST (6,424/1956, Seafire Shipping Co. SA, Greece) in fog off Ushant. The NATCREST sank and was subsequently declared a total loss.
1981: Owners became Pioneer Shipping Ltd., Monrovia, Liberia (Armada Marine SA (A.S. Manes), Piraeus, Greece) under the Greek flag.
9.1.1984: Left Osaka for demolition by mainland Chinese shipbreakers and arrived mainland China about 15.1.1984.

Rievaulx with the others of the North Yorkshire quartet was registered at Middlesbrough. *[J. and M. Clarkson]*

Ripon. [J. and M. Clarkson]

RIPON 1956-1972
O.N. 187305 10,731g 5,529n 15,100d 505'1" x 69'0" x 28'11¾"
4-cyl. 2SCSA Doxford-type oil engine by David Rowan and Co. Ltd., Glasgow; 670 x 2,320, 4,500 BHP, 11.5 knots.
18.4.1956: Launched by Lithgows Ltd., Port Glasgow (Yard No. 1085) for the North Yorkshire Shipping Co. Ltd. (Bolton Steam Shipping Co.Ltd., managers), London as RIPON.
7.1956: Completed.
9.1966: Rescued the crew of the DESCUBRIDOR (2,181/1960, Naviera Alvargonzalez SA, Gijon, Spain) which had lost her rudder in the Atlantic and towed her into Cork.
1969: Owners became Bolton Steam Shipping Co. Ltd., London.
26.5.1972: Arrived Santander for demolition. Resold to Letasa SA, Spain and used as a hulk for lightening coal-carrying bulk carriers at Santurce, Spain.

C.T. BOWRING and CO. LTD.
Bowring Steam Ship Co. Ltd. (C.T. Bowring and Co. Ltd., managers), London

TRINCULO 1957-1972
O.N. 187588 11,206g 5,819n 14,600d 504'10" x 69'4" x 27'6"
4-cyl. 2SCSA Doxford-type oil engine by Wallsend Slipway and Engineering Co. Ltd., Wallsend-on-Tyne; 670 x 2,320, 4,350 BHP, 12.5 knots.
30.1.1957: Launched by Swan Hunter and Wigham Richardson Ltd., Wallsend-on-Tyne (Yard No. 1861) for Bowring Steam Ship Co. Ltd. (C.T. Bowring and Co. Ltd., managers), London as TRINCULO.
6.1957: Completed.
1972: Sold to Walter Ritscher GmbH, West Germany for demolition, but resold to mainland Chinese shipbreakers. Renamed INCU and registered under the ownership of Atlantic Shipping Co. Ltd., Gibraltar for delivery voyage from Lübeck to Whampoa.
27.11.1972: Arrived at Whampoa for breaking up.

Trinculo. [Roy Fenton collection]

CAMPBELLS (NEWCASTLE) LTD.
Northern Mercantile and Investment Corporation Ltd. (Campbells (Newcastle) Ltd., managers), Newcastle-upon-Tyne.

DALHANNA 1957-1959
O.N. 186874 11,452g 5,912n 15,900d 504'5" x 68'6" x 29'1½"
4-cyl. 2SCSA Doxford-type oil engine by David Rowan and Co. Ltd., Glasgow; 670 x 2,320, 4,500 BHP, 11.5 knots.
20.12.1957: Launched by Lithgows Ltd., Port Glasgow (Yard No. 1109) for Northern Mercantile and Investments Corporation Ltd. (Campbells' (Newcastle) Ltd., managers), Newcastle-upon-Tyne as DALHANNA.
28.3.1958: Completed.
23.8.1958: Collided with the trawler STAXTON WYKE (427/1937, West Dock Steam Fishing Co. Ltd.) in thick fog off Flamborough Head. The STAXTON WYKE sank and five of her crew were lost.
11.1.1959: Managers became Hunting and Son Ltd., Newcastle-upon-Tyne.
21.12.1965: Owners restyled William Baird Mining Ltd., London.
1973: Sold to Silver Lake Shipping Co. SA, Panama (Stavros A. Daifos, Piraeus, Greece) for a price in excess of £350,000 and renamed SILVER ISLAND under the Greek flag.
1981: Sold to Dawlish Shipping Corporation, Monrovia, Liberia (Union Comercial Steamship Co. (Mark Scufalos), Piraeus, Greece) and renamed AMALIA.
20.10.1981: Laid up near Piraeus.
16.4.1983: Arrived at Gadani Beach for demolition by Amica Construction Works.

Above: *Dalhanna* was originally ordered as a 13,900 tonner. She was named after a farm at Dalhanna in Ayrshire which had belonged to the Campbell family since 1851. In the top photograph taken in 1958 she is at anchor in the St. Lawrence, probably waiting to load at Sept Iles. In the lower, she is arriving at Newport in August 1967 in Hunting's colours. *[Both: J. and M. Clarkson]*

CLYDE SHIPPING CO. LTD.

NEEDLES (PT) 1958-1973

O.N. 300198 6,859g 3,112n 9,250d 425'6" x 57'3" x 25'4"
3-cyl. 2SCSA Doxford-type oil engine by Wm. Doxford and Sons (Engineers) Ltd., Sunderland; 600 x 2,320, 2,600 BHP, 11.5 knots.
5.2.1958: Launched by Austin and Pickersgill Ltd., Sunderland (Yard No. 355) for the Clyde Shipping Co. Ltd., Glasgow as NEEDLES.
29.5.1958: Completed.
2.1960: Sold to Denholm Line Steamers Ltd. (J. and J. Denholm (Management) Ltd.), Glasgow and renamed WELLPARK.
12.2.1973: Arrived at Faslane for demolition by Shipbreaking Industries Ltd.
13.2.1973: Work began.

It was the practice of the Clyde Shipping Company to name its ships after lighthouses and *Needles* took hers from the lighthouse on the Isle of White. Her short career as *Needles* - she was sold to Denholms within two years - has made it difficult to find an acceptable photograph of her under her first name and below she is seen as *Wellpark*. *[J. and M. Clarkson]*

Afghanistan (top) was the first of seven ore carriers built for Common Brothers. She was unique in having kingposts forward. The photograph below of her as *Paxo* shows that she returned to the British iron ore ports later in her career. *[Top: J. and M. Clarkson; bottom: Bernard McCall]*

COMMON BROTHERS LTD

Hindustan Steam Shipping Co. Ltd. (Common Brothers Ltd., managers), Newcastle-upon-Tyne.

In 1969 the name of the management company, Common Brothers Ltd., was changed to Common Brothers (Management) Ltd.

AFGHANISTAN 1957-1972:

O.N. 186870 11,188g 5,695n 15,841d 526'3" x 69'1" x 25'8¾".
4-cyl. 2SCSA B&W-type oil engine by Harland and Wolff Ltd., Glasgow; 620 x 1,400, 4,500 BHP, 11.5 knots.
14.2.1957: Launched by Harland and Wolff Ltd., Glasgow (Yard No. 1576G) for Hindustan Steam Shipping Co. Ltd. (Common Brothers Ltd., managers), Newcastle-upon-Tyne as AFGHANISTAN.
6.1957: Completed.
1964: Owners became North Shipping Co. Ltd., Newcastle-upon-Tyne.
1966: Owners became Hindustan Steam Shipping Co. Ltd., Newcastle-upon-Tyne.
1969: Owners became Common Brothers Ltd., Newcastle-upon-Tyne.
1970: Owners became Burnside Shipping Co. Ltd., Newcastle-upon-Tyne.
1972: Sold to Compania de Naviera Levantino SA, Panama (Societa Armamento Marittimo SpA, Genoa, Italy) and renamed LEVANTINO.
1981: Sold to Hesperides Shipping Co., Panama (Medsea S.A.M., Monaco) and renamed PAXO.
14.5.1986: Arrived at Ferrol for demolition by Astano SA.
6.8.1986: Demolition commenced.

DAGHESTAN 1960-1975:

O.N. 186909 11,204g 5,666n 15,879d 525'10" x 69'0" x 28'9½"
4-cyl. 2SCSA B&W-type oil engine by Harland and Wolff Ltd., Glasgow; 620 x 1,400, 4,500 BHP, 11.5 knots.
25.5.1960: Launched by Harland and Wolff Ltd., Glasgow (Yard No. 1642G) for Hindustan Steam Shipping Co. Ltd. (Common Brothers Ltd., managers), Newcastle-upon-Tyne as DAGHESTAN.
11.1960: Completed.
1964: Owners became North Shipping Co. Ltd., Newcastle-upon-Tyne.
1969: Owners became Hindustan Steam Shipping Co. Ltd., Newcastle-upon-Tyne.
1970: Owners became Burnside Shipping Co. Ltd., Newcastle-upon-Tyne.
1973: Owners became Common Brothers Ltd., Newcastle-upon-Tyne.
1975: Sold to Sealand Carriers Corporation, Monrovia, Liberia (Ugland Management Co. A/S, Grimstad, Norway) and renamed LOVINDA under the Singapore flag.
1981: Sold to Mergui Shipping (Private) Ltd., Singapore (Planet Shipping Co. Ltd., London) and renamed MERCURY.
11.6.1982: Severely damaged aft by a fire which had broken out in her engine room when she was 60 miles south-east of Crete during a voyage from Varna to Manila.
21.6.1982: Arrived in tow at Piraeus.
29.3.1987: Arrived in tow at Aliaga to be broken up by Gursoy Gemi Sokum Ticaret A.S. It appears that she had not been repaired following the 1982 fire and she was deleted from 'Lloyd's Register' in 1984.

Vallum Shipping Co. Ltd. (Common Brothers Ltd., managers), Newcastle-upon-Tyne

IRON AGE 1958-1968
O.N. 186877 11,188g 5,697n 15,841d 526'3" x 69'1" x 28'8¾"
4-cyl. 2SCSA B&W-type oil engine by Harland and Wolff Ltd., Glasgow; 620 x 1,400, 4,500 BHP, 11.5 knots.
20.1.1958: Launched by Harland and Wolff Ltd., Glasgow (Yard No. 1577G) for Vallum Shipping Co. Ltd. (Common Brothers Ltd., managers), Newcastle-upon-Tyne as IRON AGE.
5.1958: Completed.
1968: Sold to Compania de Naviera Nino SA, Panama (Societa Armamento Marittimo in Nome Collettivo, Genoa, Italy) and renamed NINO.
1969: Owners became Navale Spartivento SpA, Cagliari, Italy (Societa Armamento Marittimo SpA, Genoa, Italy) and renamed ONORATO.
1981: Sold to Alpha Orionis SA, Panama (Medsea SAM, Monaco) and renamed HERAKLIA.
1988: Sold to Rover Marine SA, Liberia and renamed HERA under the St Vincent flag.
14.10.1988: Arrived at Port Alang for demolition by Madhav Industrial Corporation.

IRON BARQUE 1960-1970
O.N. 186902 10.950g 4,530n 15,970d 516'7" x 69'1" x 28'8¼"
4-cyl. 2SCSA Doxford-type oil engine by North Eastern Marine Engineering Co. Ltd., Wallsend-upon-Tyne; 670 x 2,320, 4,400 BHP, 11.5 knots.
11.3.1960: Launched by Austin and Pickersgill Ltd., Sunderland (Yard No. 364) for Vallum Shipping Co. Ltd. (Common Brothers Ltd., managers), Newcastle-upon-Tyne as IRON BARQUE.
5.1960: Completed.
1970: Sold to Landmo Shipping Corporation Ltd., Monrovia (Landmo Shipping Services Ltd. (J.J. Ugland), London) and renamed MAHINDA under the Singapore flag.
10.3.1987: Left Karachi for Port Alang for demolition by Bharat Shipbreakers Corporation.
1.4.1987: Work commenced.

IRON CROWN 1960-1971
O.N. 186912 11,125g 4,512n 15.912d 518'0" x 69'1" x 28'9¼"
4-cyl. 2SCSA Doxford-type oil engine by Scotts' Shipbuilding and Engineering Co. Ltd., Greenock; 670 x 2,320, 4,400 BHP, 11.5 knots.
21.11.1960: Launched by Scotts' Shipbuilding and Engineering Co. Ltd., Greenock (Yard No. 683) for Vallum Shipping Co. Ltd. (Common Brothers Ltd., managers), Newcastle-upon-Tyne as IRON CROWN.
1.1961: Completed.
1971: Sold to Whitwill Cole and Co. Ltd., Bristol (W.A. Souter and Co. Ltd., Newcastle-upon-Tyne, managers) and renamed SCOTTISH WASA.
1975: Owners became Spanocean Line Ltd. (Whitco Marine Services Ltd., London) (W.A. Souter and Co. Ltd., Newcastle-upon-Tyne, managers).
1977: Sold to Thomson Shipping Co. Ltd., Monrovia, Liberia (Const. Tsamopoulos, Piraeus, Greece) and renamed JEANNIE under the Greek flag.
1979: Owners became Lansdowne Shipping Co. Ltd., Monrovia, Liberia (Const. Tsamopoulos, Piraeus, Greece).
1985: Sold to Amesa International Shipping and Finance Ltd., Gibraltar (Anro Maritime Enterprises SA, Piraeus, Greece) and renamed AMESA DYO.
28.4.1986: Arrived at Gadani Beach for demolition by Murtaza Enterprises Ltd.
3.5.1986: Work commenced.

A quartet of Common Brothers' ore carriers. From top to bottom: *Daghestan, Iron Age, Iron Barque,* and *Iron Crown.* The Vallum ships carried different colours from the *Afghanistan* and *Daghestan. [All: J. and M. Clarkson]*

IRON HORSE 1960-1970
O.N. 186907 11,128g 4,523n 15,892d 518'0" x 69'1" x 28'9¹/4"
4 cyl. 2SCSA Doxford-type oil engine by Scotts' Shipbuilding and Engineering Co. Ltd., Greenock; 670 x 2,320, 4,400 BHP, 11.5 knots.
11.5.1960: Launched by Scotts' Shipbuilding and Engineering Co. Ltd., Greenock (Yard No. 682) for Vallum Shipping Co. Ltd. (Common Brothers Ltd., managers), Newcastle-upon-Tyne as IRON HORSE.
11.1960: Completed.
21.9.1962: Collided with Mersey Docks and Harbour Board pilot vessel, EDMUND GARDNER (701/1953), in the River Mersey. The EDMUND GARDNER sustained extensive damage to her upper works and the IRON HORSE was also damaged.
1970: Sold to Aspidoforous Compania Naviera SA, Panama (Empros Lines Shipping Co. Special SA, Piraeus, Greece) and renamed ASPIDOFOROS under the Greek flag.
1976: Owners became Ebony Co. Ltd., Greece (Empros Lines Shipping Co. Special SA, Piraeus, Greece).
8.5.1982: Laid up at Piraeus.
29.11.1984: Arrived at Aliaga for demolition by Cukurova Celik Endustrisi A.S. in tow from Piraeus.

Completing the Common Brothers sequence are *Iron Horse* (above) and *Iron Ore* (below). *[Both: J. and M. Clarkson]*

IRON ORE 1959-1969
O.N. 186895 10,950g 4,530n 15,970d 516'7" x 69'1" x 28'8¹/4"
4-cyl. 2SCSA Doxford-type oil engine by North Eastern Marine Engineering Co. Ltd., Wallsend-on-Tyne; 670 x 2,320, 4,400 BHP, 12 knots.
8.7.1959: Launched by Austin and Pickersgill Ltd., Sunderland (Yard No. 363) for Vallum Shipping Co. Ltd. (Common Brothers Ltd., managers), Newcastle-upon-Tyne as IRON ORE.
10.1959: Completed.
1969: Sold to Compania de Naviera Siroco SA, Panama (Societa Armamento Marittimo in Nome Collettivo, Genoa, Italy) and renamed SIROCO under the Liberian flag.
1981: Sold to Volcano Shipping SA, Panama (Medsea SAM, Monaco) and renamed SKYROS.
1985: Owners became Medore Shipping Co. SA, Panama (Medsea SAM, Monaco) and renamed GAMBOA.
19.11.1986: Arrived Aliaga for demolition by Yazici Gemi Bokum Ticaret.
6.1986: Work commenced.

Below: *Dukesgarth. [J. and M. Clarkson]*

WM. CORY AND SON LTD.
St. Denis Shipping Co. Ltd. (Wm. Cory and Son Ltd., managers), London

DUKESGARTH 1961-1976
O.N. 302785 10,760g 4,622n 15,623d 510'8" x 70'3" x 28'0"
4-cyl. 2SCSA Doxford-type oil engine by North Eastern Marine Engineering Co. Ltd., Wallsend-upon-Tyne; 670 x 2,320, 4,400 BHP, 12.5 knots.
13.4.1961: Launched by Blyth Drydock and Shipbuilding Co. Ltd., Blyth (Yard No. 376) for St. Denis Shipping Co. Ltd. (Wm. Cory and Son Ltd., managers), London as DUKESGARTH.
9.1961: Completed.
1974: Managers became Ocean Transport and Trading Ltd., London.
1976: Sold to Pothitos Shipping Co. SA, Panama (E. Pothitos, E. Koutsofios and others, Piraeus, Greece) and renamed MICHALIS under the Greek flag.
1980: Owners became Taxiarchis Shipping Enterprises Maritime Co. SA, Panama (E. Pothitos, E. Koutsofios and others, Piraeus, Greece), and renamed TAXIARCHIS under the Greek flag.
6.8.1982: Lad up at Eleusis.
1984: Owners became Eva Shipping Co. Ltd., Valletta, Malta (E. Koutsofios, Piraeus, Greece).
18.4.1984: Arrived at Port Alang for demolition by Shirdi Steel Traders.
14.5.1984: Work commenced.

KNIGHTSGARTH 1960-1975
O.N. 302571 10,760g 4,625n 15,376d 518'0" x 70'2" x 28'0"
4-cyl. 2SCSA Doxford-type oil engine by North Eastern Marine Engineering Co. Ltd., Wallsend-upon-Tyne; 670 x 2,320, 4,400 BHP, 12.5 knots.
20.7.1960: Launched by Blyth Drydock and Shipbuilding Co. Ltd., Blyth (Yard No. 375) for St. Denis Shipping Co. Ltd. (Wm. Cory and Sons Ltd., managers), London as KNIGHTSGARTH.
2.1961: Completed.
2.11.1973: Damaged in collision with MAIPO (10,869/1966, Compania Sud-Americana de Vapores, Chile) whilst berthed at Birkenhead.
1974: Managers became Ocean Transport and Trading Ltd., London.
1975: Sold to Patmos Shipping Co. SA, Panama (Canopus Shipping SA) (Andreas and George Kyrtatas, Athens, Greece) and renamed THEOSKEPASTI.
1977: Owners became Theagenis Maritime SA, Panama (Canopus Shipping SA (Andreas and George Kyrtatas, Athens, Greece) under the Greek flag.
12.11.1986: Arrived Aliaga for demolition by Nigdeliler AS in tow from Piraeus where she had been laid up for some time.

Cory's ore carriers had names ending *-garth* in the style of the company's subsidiary, Rea, better known as tug owners but who had once owned colliers. This is *Knightsgarth. [J. and M. Clarkson]*

MONKSGARTH 1959-1977
O.N. 301116 10,760g 4,625n 15,386d 510'8" x 70'3" x 28'0"
4-cyl. 2SCSA Doxford-type oil engine by North Eastern Marine Engineering Co. Ltd., Wallsend-upon-Tyne; 670 x 2,320, 4,400 BHP, 12.5 knots.
1.12.1959: Launched by Blyth Drydock and Shipbuilding Co. Ltd., Blyth (Yard No. 371) for St. Denis Shipping Co. Ltd. (Wm. Cory and Sons Ltd., managers), London as MONKSGARTH.
4.1960: Completed.
1974: Managers became Ocean Transport and Trading Ltd., London.
1977: Sold to Compania Kifissia SA, Panama (E. Pothitos, E. Koutsofios and others, Piraeus, Greece) and renamed DAPO SAILOR under the Greek flag.
27.11.1983: Arrived Karachi for demolition by Sunrise Ship Breakers.

Monksgarth.

Queensgarth in South Wales. *[J. and M. Clarkson]*

QUEENSGARTH 1959-1977
O.N. 300996 10,762g 4,626n 15,386d 510'8" x 70'3" x 28'0"
4-cyl. 2SCSA Doxford-type oil engine by North Eastern Marine Engineering Co. Ltd., Wallsend-upon-Tyne; 670 x 2,320, 4,440 BHP, 12.5 knots.
7.5.1959: Launched by Blyth Drydock and Shipbuilding Co. Ltd., Blyth (Yard No.370) for St. Denis Shipping Co. Ltd. (Wm. Cory and Sons Ltd., managers), London as QUEENSGARTH.
9.1959: Completed.
1974: Managers became Ocean Transport and Trading Ltd., London.
1977: Sold to Compania Nida SA, Panama (Dapo Shipping SA, Panama) (N.A. Davaris, Piraeus, Greece) and renamed DAPO STAR under the Greek flag.
1981: Sold to Australind Steam Shipping Co. Ltd., London (Atwood Australind Drilling Co., Singapore) and renamed AUSTRALIND.
23.9.1981: Arrived Singapore to be converted into a drillship by Keppel Shipyard, gross tonnage became 10,609.
1982: Transferred to Hong Kong registry.
1982: Owners became Kepdrill International Inc, Panama (Atwood Australind Drilling Co., Singapore) and renamed ENIWETOK.
1985: Renamed FIVE STAR.
1989: Sold to K/S Stardrill, Oslo (J.O. Odfjell A/S, Kokstad, Norway) and renamed STARDRILL under the Liberia flag.
11.12.1992: Arrived Alang for demolition by I.M. Industries. She was listed as having been sold by St. Vincent flag owners.
28.12.1992: Work commenced.

CREST SHIPPING CO. LTD.

ORECREST (PT) 1958-1968
O.N. 199464 6,903g 2,696n 9,150d 427'0" x 57'3" x 25' 4¾"
3-cyl. 2SCSA Doxford-type oil engine by Fairfield Shipbuilding and Engineering Co. Ltd., Port Glasgow; 600 x 2,320 2,500 BHP, 10.5 knots.
9.4.1958: Launched by Lithgows Ltd., Port Glasgow (Yard No. 1123) for Crest Shipping Co. Ltd., London as ORECREST.
6.1958: Completed.
1968: Sold to Golden Sea Shipping Corporation, Monrovia, Liberia (C.T. Chu, Taipei) and renamed GOLDEN SEA.
1971: Owners became the Golden Elephant Shipping Corporation, Monrovia, Liberia (C.T. Chu, Taipei) and renamed GOLDEN ELEPHANT.
9.5.1973: Arrived Kaohsiung for demolition by Kaohsiung Steel Corporation.
13.7.1973: Work commenced.

CURRIE LINE LTD.

GOTHLAND (L) 1961-1977
O.N. 303456 16,664g 8,543n 24,923d 595'2" x 74'0" x 31'11½"
5-cyl. 2SCSA Burmeister & Wain-type oil engine by J.G. Kincaid and Co. Ltd., Greenock; 620 x 1,400, 5,400 BHP, 11 knots.
25.9.1961: Launched by Lithgows Ltd., Port Glasgow (Yard No. 1138) for Currie Line Ltd., Glasgow as GOTHLAND.
12.1961: Completed.
1977: Sold to Compania Sydenham SA, Panama (Dapo Shipping SA, Panama) (N.A. Davaris, Piraeus, Greece) and renamed DAPO SKY under the Greek flag.
1977: Owners became Compania Nea Smyrni SA, Panama (Dapo Shipping SA, Panama) (N.A. Davaris, Piraeus, Greece).
22.8.1978: Suffered extensive damage to her superstructure when fire broke out in her engine room whilst proceeding down the Clyde outward bound from Glasgow to Puerto Ordez.
25.8.1978: Returned to Glasgow for examination and found to be beyond repair. Sold to Shipbreaking Industries Ltd., Faslane for demolition.
23.4.1979: Arrived Faslane.

The *Gothland* was named after a region of Sweden. *[J. and M. Clarkson]*

Although in homogenous groups, the ore carriers were by no means all identical. *Orecrest,* the solitary example owned by Crest Shipping, seems modelled on *Ormsary* but has a distinctly styled funnel, more accommodation aft, and a more substantial signal mast on the bridge. *Orecrest's* colour scheme changed during her career, as the top two photographs illustrate. Frustratingly, it is just not possible to read the inscription on the bow crest in the upper photograph

The bottom photograph shows her in later life as *Golden Elephant.* Now mounted between the pair of holds are two cranes which appear to have turned her into a general cargo carrier. *[Top: J. and M. Clarkson; middle: Fotoflite incorporating Skyfotos; bottom: Foxley]*

RS DALGLIESH LTD.
Watergate Steam Ship Co.Ltd.(RS Dalgliesh Ltd., managers), Newcastle-upon-Tyne.

The Watergate Steam Ship Co. Ltd.was originally owned by R.S. Dalgliesh Ltd., but in 1969 the company was acquired by the Lonhro group. In 1974 it was sold to Kristian Jebsen (UK) Ltd. Management of the company remained with R.S. Dalgliesh Ltd. at all times.

PENNYWORTH 1958-1973
O.N. 186882 10,978g 4,545n 15,400d 505'0" x 68'1" x 28'10¾"
4-cyl. 2SCSA Doxford-type oil engine by Hawthorn Leslie (Engineering) Ltd., Newcastle-upon-Tyne; 670 x 2,320, 4,450 BHP, 11.5 knots.
2.6.1958: Launched by Smith's Dock Co. Ltd., Middlesbrough (Yard No. 1251) for Watergate Steam Ship Co. Ltd. (R.S. Dalgliesh Ltd., managers), Newcastle-upon-Tyne as PENNYWORTH.
10.1958: Completed.
1973: Sold to Rio Santo Shipping Co. Ltd., Famagusta, Cyprus (Seven Seas Maritime Ltd.) (B. and S. Kalamotusis and P.E. Kollakis), London for £275,000 and renamed KAPPA UNITY.
1974: Sold to Newland SA, Panama (Overland Trust Bank, Lugano, Switzerland) and renamed NEWLAND.
1975: Sold to Gino Gardella, Genoa, Italy and renamed PISOLO.
1983: Sold to Zosma SpA di Navigazione, Milan (Gino Gardella SpA, Genoa, Italy).
12.7.1982: Laid up at La Spezia.
4.9.1983: Demolition commenced at La Spezia by Cantiere de Lotti SpA.

RAVENSWORTH (PT) 1960-1975
O.N. 186911 6,805g 2,692n 9,740d 425'6" x 57'5" x 25'7"
4-cyl. 2SCSA Doxford-type oil engine by North Eastern Marine Engineering Co. Ltd., Wallsend-upon-Tyne; 600 x 2,320, 2,600 BHP, 11.5 knots.
6.10.1960: Launched by Austin and Pickersgill Ltd., Sunderland (Yard No. 365) for Watergate Steam Ship Co. Ltd. (R.S. Dalgliesh Ltd., managers), Newcastle-upon-Tyne as RAVENSWORTH.
12.1960: Completed.
1975: Sold to Houlder Line Ltd. (Houlder Brothers and Co. Ltd., managers), London.
1975: Sold to Flexservice NV, Willemstad, Netherlands Antilles (Ugland Management Co. A/S, Grimstad, Norway) and renamed FLEXSERVICE 1.
22.11.1975: Arrived Kristiansand for conversion to a pipe layer by Kristiansands Mek Versted A/S. Gross tonnage now 5,445.
1986: Transferred to Panama flag.
1997: Sold to Deepsea Ltd.SA (CAPCO Trust IOM Ltd., Douglas, Isle of Man) (Coflexip International SA, Paris, France), remaining under Panama flag.
15.1.2001: Sold to Eckhardt Marine GmbH, Germany and renamed SERVICE under the Cambodian flag.
14.2.2001: Arrived at Port Alang for demolition.

Pennyworth (above) and *Ravensworth* (below) carried traditional Dalgleish names. *[Both: J. and M. Clarkson]*

Two fine panoramic views of Malta show the former *Pennyworth* as *Kappa Unity* (above) and newly renamed in 1974 (below). As can be seen, the new name appeared on her stern, at least initially, as *New Land,* but registers refer to it as *Newland,* and some editions of 'Lloyd's Register' give *Newlands. [Both: Michael Cassar]*

IMMO-RAGNAR
Clyde Shipbuilding and Engineering Co. Ltd., Port Glasgow; 1903, 2,300gt, 300 feet
T.3-cyl. by Clyde Shipbuilding and Engineering Co. Ltd., Port Glasgow
One of our oldest Finns from the fifties has the extensive deck cargo of timber so often seen on these ships. Her career began on the Clyde with local ownership by the Hermia Steamship Co. Ltd. (James Neil, manager) as *Hermia,* continuing under British ownership as *Capelcourt* from 1917 and *Lynntown* from 1919. In January 1932 she was sold to A/B R. Nordström & Co. O/Y of Lovisa who first renamed her *Inga.* In 1936 the owners wanted to give this name to another vessel, and she became *Immo Ragnar,* as seen in this post-war view. Quite what her war service involved is not known, but she survived, and steamed on until September 1956 when she arrived at Grays in Essex to be broken up by T.W. Ward Ltd. *[Fotoflite incorporating Skyfotos]*

FINNS IN THE FIFTIES

Roy Fenton and Hubert Hall

Like the Spanish fleet (see *Record* 17), the Finnish merchant navy in the 1950s was a delight to the enthusiast because of the many ageing, often still steam-powered, ships which it comprised. Finland had fought an extremely valiant war of liberation against its mighty neighbour, but was labelled as an 'enemy' when the USSR joined the Allied cause. Hence, when Finland finally succumbed to the Russian steamroller, it lost some of its existing fleet. Although Finland had an active shipbuilding industry, efforts in post-war years were directed towards providing 'reparations' to the USSR. Even when this ended in 1952, a series of trade agreements saw Finnish ship production orientated towards Russian needs. As a result, Finland's fleet in the 1950s was an interesting mixture of mostly ageing steamers and motor vessels.

Adding to the attraction of Finnish ships were the deliciously foreign titles of the owning companies, at least for those with access to 'Lloyds Register' who could further their knowledge of the ships by looking up such details. The closest relations to the Finnish language are Hungarian and Turkish, possibly being the survivors of a language family squeezed between the Slavic tongues to the east and the Latin-derived languages to the west. Finland is bilingual, with Swedish co-existing alongside Finnish, and many companies had a Finnish and a Swedish name, e.g. Suomen Höyrylaiva Oy and Finska Ångfartygs Ab. The linguistic twists, the habitual timber cargoes carried, and the evidence of encounters between ice and hulls, gave vintage Finnish ships a romantic appeal as coming from a far northern world of forests and frozen lakes.

This feature recalls some of the vintage Finns that could be seen in the fifties, presented in roughly chronological order of building date.

BALTIC (top)
Schiffswerft von Henry Koch, Lübeck; 1898, 1,077gt, 202 feet
T. 3-cyl. by Blohm & Voss, Hamburg
It is fitting that the oldest ship shown here is a representative of the senior Finnish shipping company, Finska Ångfartygs Ab (Finland Steamship Co. Ltd., for short FAA or EFFOA), founded in 1883 to operate a steamer service from Helsinki to the UK. *Baltic* was built for Helsingfors Ångfartygs Ab with both passenger and cargo accommodation, but the former was removed when her owners amalgamated with FAA in 1920. In her guise as a pure cargo steamer *Baltic* lasted remarkably well, and was not delivered to Finnish breakers, at Mathiledal, until October 1960. *[Hubert Hall collection]*

RAGUNDA (below)
Hellerups Skibsvaerft & Maskinbyggeri, Hellerup; 1901, 1,629gt, 190 feet
T. 3-cyl. by Dansk Maskinfabrik, Copenhagen
Ragunda carried only two names in her 54 years, but had a number of owners and managers. As *Lena* she was built for Norwegians, was sold to Sweden in 1915, becoming *Ragunda* in 1916. *Ragunda* passed to Finland in May 1933, and in 1940 its owners were acquired by the company whose colours she is in here, A/B Nordström & Co. Oy of Lovisa. With subtle changes in the name of these owners, she steamed on until 1955, when she arrived at Dover on 26th November to be broken up by Dover Industries Ltd.

Note that *Ragunda* is carrying what is probably a deck cargo of coke, but for a much more spectacular example of this cargo, see 'Every picture tells a story' on page 143 of this issue. *[A. Duncan]*

AXEL (above)
Howaldtswerke, Kiel; 1904, 950gt, 213 feet
T. 3-cyl. by Howaldtswerke, Kiel
Uniquely amongst the veterans shown here, *Axel* carried just one name throughout its 53 years, although like the others it changed owner and flag. She was built for Holm & Wonsild of Copenhagen, who sold her to owners in Rauma, Finland in 1928. In 1940 *Axel* passed to the Nautic Steamship Co. Ltd. managed by John Lindblom of Åbo/Turkü, and was still with this owner when photographed post-war. She was delivered to breakers in Antwerp in August 1957.

Axel represents another variant on the engines-amidships small Baltic tramp layout, one popular in Germany with just three holds and a long raised-quarterdeck. *[Hubert Hall collection]*

HILDEGAARD (below)
Richardson, Duck and Co., Stockton; 1906, 2,468, 313 feet
T. 3-cyl. by Blair and Co. Ltd., Stockton
Hildegard is a survivor of the classic British tramp steamers of the early twentieth century, although her bridge, and perhaps other parts of her anatomy, have undergone surgery.

Her original name was *Eda,* for the eponymous Eda Steamship Co. Ltd. managed by Burdick and Cook of London. She had several other British owners and managers, but not until 1919 did one of these rename her, as *Butetown.* Owners were now the Town Line (London) Ltd., which somewhat contradictorily was managed in Cardiff by Harrison, Sons and Co. As David and Geraint Jenkins write in their excellent 'Cardiff Shipowners', these Harrisons were a very successful firm of Cardiff shipowners, coal exporters and coal owners, but with an expensively-acquired fleet got into deep trouble with the post-First World War recession. *Butetown* was one of their many ships to go in an ultimately-doomed attempt to rescue the Harrison's empire. In 1924 Boe & Pedersen of Oslo picked her up for what was certainly a bargain price, and renamed her *Hildegaard.*

Her name remained unchanged when she was bought by a member of the Lundqvist family of Mariehamn in 1935. She remained in the ownership of Rederi A/B Hildegaard until 1960 when a fire at Gdynia in February put an end to her long career, and she was sent to Odense for breaking up by H.I. Hansen. *[Hubert Hall collection]*

BORE IV (above)
Burmeister & Wain, Copenhagen; 1907, 1,708gt, 280 feet
T. 3-cyl. by Burmeister & Wain, Copenhagen
Despite their string of unimaginative names, the ships of Ångfartygs Ab Bore of Turkü were an interestingly mixed lot, including one attractive two-funnelled ferry steamer, the *Bore* (3,475/1960). The former British tramp *Bore IX* appeared in *Record 22,* and here is *Bore IV,* in a classically photogenic location beneath one of the majestic bridges spanning the Kiel Canal. She has a very neatly stowed cargo of timber no doubt destined for a port in western Europe, quite possibly London.

Built in Denmark she had a variety of Danish owners, first as *Olaf,* then as *Loly Jensen* from 1915, *Strandholm* from 1919, and *Skotland* from 1923. Adopted on her acquisition by Rederi Bore A/B in 1936, *Bore IV* was the ship's fifth name, but not her last. In 1960 *Bore IV* she was sold to other Finnish owners and renamed *Bodal* until broken up in 1962. *[Foto Renard, Kiel; Hubert Hall collection]*

TORA (below)
A/S Sörlandet Skibsvaerft, Fevig; 1919, 1,815, 265 feet
T. 3-cyl. by A/S Fredriksstad M/V, Fredriksstad
Tora is the classic Baltic freighter as many remember her; with cargo gear at the extremities of the holds to maximise space for a timber deck cargo, tall, straight funnel smoking freely, and - when light - a barely submerged propellor churning the water.

Her 45-year history was complex but not unusual. Built as *Antares* for Erik Brodins Rederi A/B of Sweden, in 1922 she was renamed *Eda* for owners in Christiania (later Oslo). She returned to Swedish ownership in 1926 without change of name, and in 1934 began a long period under the Finnish flag as *Karin Thorden.* Owner was Gustaf B. Thordén, who came to Finland from Sweden in 1923 but went back in 1944 when his adopted country's future was unclear. In 1955 the ship took the name *Tora* for Red A/B Tora, managed by Carsten Danielson and Son of Helsingfors, a Dane who came to Finland: note his initial D on the funnel. *Tora* was broken up at Lübeck by Alnwick Harmstorf early in 1964. *[Roy Fenton collection]*

SAIMAA (top)
Eriksbergs Mek. Verks. A/B, Gothenburg; 1922, 1,824g 300 feet
Oil engine 4SCSA 6-cyl. by A/B Gotaverken, Gothenburg
Like so many Finnish ships, *Saimaa* accumulated a lot of history in her 45-year career.

A relatively early motorship, she was laid down for Rederi A/B Svenska Lloyd and launched for them as *Trinacria,* but sold before completion in September 1922 to other Swedish owners, for operation by Svenska Orient Line as *Erland.*

She was bought by FAA and renamed *Saimaa* in April 1937, and in 1940 was their only ship fortunate enough to remain outside the Baltic, trading to South America on charter to Grace Lines. Once the USA entered the war, Finnish ships were technically enemies, and soon after the arrival of *Saimaa* at New York from Cuba on 26th December 1941 she was seized and taken into the ownership of the US War Shipping Administration, who placed her under the Panama flag as *Yemassee.* She had a variety of managers, including the Isbrandtsen Steamship Co., and seems to have worked hard throughout the war, until laid up in October 1945.

FAA reclaimed her in New York in March 1947, and after repairs *Saimaa* sailed for Finland to resume service, as in the accompanying photograph.

The final chapter of her story began in March 1964 when she was sold to an owner in Trieste who registered her in Panama as *Taitu* under the ownership of Claramar SA. On 19th October 1967 she had sailed from the port of Marina di Carrara which serves Italy's marble industry with a cargo destined for Port Sudan, which - with the closure of the Suez Canal - had to be taken round the Cape. But hardly had she cleared Italian waters when the 45-year old motor vessel foundered off the southern point of Sicily. *[Hubert Hall collection]*

ENSO (middle) and **HAKUNI** (bottom)
A.G. Neptun, Rostock; 1927, 1,901gt, 279 feet
T. 3-cyl. by A.G. Neptun, Rostock
Being built for Baltic trading, it is not surprising that several German ships featured in the Finnish fleet. *Ernst Brockleman* had been built at Rostock for local owners, again exemplifying the German predilection for long raised quarter deck, this time with masts placed centrally between the holds. In May 1945, when most undamaged, or repairable, tonnage was being stripped from German ports, she was taken as a war reparation in Flensburg and became *Empire Concession,* her name beginning *Con-* indicating she had been condemned as a prize of war. She found a British buyer in 1947, Blandy Brothers and Co. Ltd. of London, who may well have run her in the timber trade, giving her the name *Brazen Head.*

In 1950 she was acquired by Enso Gutzeit O/Y of Kotka, a company managed by O/Y Finnlines, and renamed *Enso.* In 1959 *Enso* was sold to Raumanmeri O/Y (E. Fagerstrom, manager) of Rauma and renamed *Hakuni,* as which she is seen here, probably in the Thames Estuary, on 24th May 1959.

In 1966 she took her last name *Isla del Rey,* as which she was registered in Panama. This may have been for no more than her last voyage to the breakers, as she was scrapped at Alicante in Spain during June 1966. *[Roy Fenton collection; John G. Callis]*

ARUBA
Swan, Hunter and Wigham Richardson Ltd., Wallsend-on-Tyne; 1931, 10,382, 493 feet
6-cyl. 2SCSA oil engines by Wallsend Slipway and Engineering Co. Ltd., Wallsend-on-Tyne

Aruba was a motor tanker, although one would not guess it from the smoke produced in the photograph of her below alongside a tank farm in icy conditions.

She had been built as *Pan Aruba,* one of a series for Leif Höegh of Oslo. This Norwegian had realised the potential in oil transportation whilst working for Wilhelm Wilhelmsen, and established his own shipowning company in June 1927. Remarkably, just four years later he was taking delivery of what were some of the world's largest motor tankers. *Pan Aruba, Pan Scandia* and *Pan Europe* were built by Swan, Hunter and chartered to Standard Oil of New Jersey. Leif Höegh went on to become one of Norway's foremost shipowners, as well as tankers operating dry cargo ships in tramp and cargo liner trades.

In 1948 *Pan Aruba* came into Finnish ownership, simply dropping the 'Pan' to become *Aruba.* Joint owners were Hans von Rettig and A/B Wilh. Bensow, who registered *Aruba* under the title Rederibolget Re-Be, a name conjoining their own names. As if there was some disagreement as to whose name should take priority, *Aruba's* funnel carries these owners initials in reverse order, BR.

Aruba was broken up by Brodospas at Split, Yugoslavia in 1959. Her near sisters *Pan Scandia* and *Pan Europe* also survived the war and, after short careers under the German and Panama flags, respectively, were broken up in 1954. *[Top: Fotoflite incorporating Skyfotos; bottom: Hubert Hall collection]*

WANDA (above)
Nya Varvs. Öresund, Landskrona; 1932, 1,568gt, 275 feet
T. 3-cyl. by Nya Varvs. Öresund, Landskrona
As the most industrialised country in Scandinavia, with abundant supplies of iron ore, it is not surprising that Sweden was the leading shipbuilding nation in Scandinavia, and many of its products were represented in the Finnish fleet of the 1950s.

A ship called *Wanda,* seen here in South Wales, has an appearance which belies her years, as she is a comparative youngster from 1932 despite her uncompromisingly severe lines. A minor feature are her solid bulwarks, which run almost the length of her hull, but are replaced by rails around the stern and for a short distance forward of her first hold, this presumably being to facilitate handing of ropes.

Built as *Inger,* she was renamed *Wanda* in 1955 for Ab Baltic Lloyd Line Ltd. Oy, Helsinki, managed by Herbert Janhonen. The letter H on her funnel (and on the *Otava,* below) signifies Helsingin Lloyd Oy, also managed by Herbert Janhone. This company and A/B Baltic Lloyd Line were amalgamated in January 1959.

In 1965 *Wanda* was sold to Greek owners who put her under the Panama flag as *Captain Frangos.* Her end came on 19th February 1968 when she was in collision off Canakkale whilst carrying a cargo of asphalt from Albania to Varna. *[J. and M. Clarkson]*

KAARINA (below)
Nylands Verks, Oslo; 1938, 1,397gt, 272 feet
C. 2-cyl. with low-pressure turbine by Nylands Verks, Oslo
A fond memory of ship watching on the Mersey at the very end of the 1950s is of the frequent visits of Nordström's *Kaarina.* Relatively young in comparison with the veterans seen here, she was still recognisably a Baltic type, although concessions to modernity included a nicely raked bow and shaping of the bridge plating. Internally, her compound two-cylinder engines were augmented by low-pressure turbines.

She had been built at Oslo as *Dr. Heinrich Wiegand* for Argo Reederei Richard Adler & Co., Bremen. In 1940 she was taken over by the German navy, although the name she was given, *Norwegentransporter,* does not appear in post-war 'Lloyd's Registers' as an ex-name. As a German prize, she was handed over the US Maritime Commission in July 1946, although she was damaged by fire in October 1946. In 1948 she was sold to Seatrade Corporation of New York, but in November 1949 returned to Europe, becoming the Danish owned *Else Basse.* In August 1953, she suffered a fire in her machinery off the US coast, and after being abandoned was taken in tow by the *LST 287.* She returned to Copenhagen for repair, but this accident may have precipitated her disposal, as in May 1954 she was exchanged with A/B R. Nordström & Co. O/Y of Lovisa for another *Kaarina* (439/1949). Renaming the steamer *Kaarina,* Nordstrom ran her under various owning companies until May 1968 when she was delivered to Hamburg to be scrapped by Eckhardt & Co. GmbH. *[John G. Callis]*

OTAVA (above)
Helsingborgs Varfs. A/B, Helsingborg; 1942, 1,593gt, 296 feet.
T. 3-cyl. with exhaust turbine by Helsingborgs Varfs. A/B, Helsingborg
The wooden bridge front of *Otava* is a sight to gladden the heart. Interesting that time and money could be found for this indulgence in wartime Sweden.

The steamer was built as *A. Th. Jonasson* and renamed *Helios* for other Swedish owners in 1950, taking the name *Otava* in 1959 when acquired by A/B Baltic Lloyd Line Ltd. O/Y, Helsinki as seen here (see also *Wanda*). In 1967 Herbert Janhonen, who managed her, decided to sell off his fleet, and *Otava* went off to the Mediterranean as *Maddalena* for owners in Torre del Greco. She was quickly sold on to other Italian owners, and as *Generoso* was owned in Venice, Marina di Carrara and Bari before being broken up at Brindisi in October 1975. *[J. and M. Clarkson]*

DAFNY (below)
Burmeister & Wain, Copenhagen; 1941-1943, 4,463gt, 382 feet
5-cyl. 2SCSA oil engine by Burmeister & Wain, Copenhagen
A motorship, and one which did not come to Finland until the early 1960s, the *Dafny* is still of interest for her unusual layout, with three holds all served by derricks worked from kingposts, with one hold comprehensively splitting the superstructure. Note too the prominent winch house built out from the bridge front.

She was built in Denmark as *Vedby* for Danish account during the Second World War, her protracted construction being a consequence of the German occupation. Danish owners were Motortramp A/S. In 1962 she was renamed *Dafny* in the ownership of Rederi A/B Sally, managed by Algot Johansson of Mariehamn, a company which later became famous for its ferry operations. *Dafny* was sold to Panama owners in 1975, but tramped on as *Marlin II* until 1980 when she was broken up at Marin. Despite being built under wartime conditions, the ship had a lengthy career. *[J.K. Byass]*

Fleet in Focus
NORTH PACIFIC COAST LINE Part 2
David Burrell

Nederlandsch-Amerikaansche Stoomvaart Maatschappij N.V., Rotterdam

1. DINTELDIJK 1922-1944
9,398g 5,814n 11,968d. 485.6 x 62.3 x 35.8 feet.
Two 8-cyl. 4SCSA Burmeister & Wain-type oil engines by Harland and Wolff Ltd., Glasgow driving twin screws; 5,000 BHP, 13 knots.
1.9.1921: Launched by Harland and Wolff Ltd, Glasgow (Yard No. 515).
2.1922: Completed for Nederlandsch-Amerikaansche Stoomvaart Maatschappij, Rotterdam as DINTELDIJK
10.5.1940: Seized by German forces at Rotterdam.
27.9.1944: Scuttled in the Nieuwe Waterweg above Maassluis and broke in two.
2.1946: Wreck blown up to clear waterway.

2. DRECHTDIJK 1923-1940
9,338g 5,808n 11,968d 485.5 x 62.3 x 35.5 feet.
Two 8-cyl. 4SCSA Burmeister & Wain-type oil engines by Harland and Wolff Ltd., Glasgow driving twin screws; 5,000 BHP, 13 knots.
24.10.1922: Launched by Harland and Wolff Ltd., Greenock (Yard No. 593).
3.1923: Completed for Nederlandsch-Amerikaansche Stoomvaart Maatschappij, Rotterdam as DRECHTDIJK.
9.8.1940: Seized by German forces at Rotterdam.
12.3.1941: Taken to Swinemunde to become transport RO13 for Operation Sealion. Operated by Unterweser Reederei A.G., Bremen as RÜSSELSHEIM.
17.2.1945: Mined one mile east of Swinemunde.
18.2.1945: Beached on fire in position 53.56 north by 14.17 east.
12.3.1945: Bombed by Allied aircraft.
24.12.1945: Returned to owners, towed from Kiel to Rotterdam.
30.11.1947: Sold to Van Heyghen Frères, Ghent for breaking up.
5.12.1947: Work commenced.

3. DELFTDIJK/DONGEDYK 1930-1966
10,220g 6,385n 490.9 x 64.7 x 34.1 feet.
1952: 10,942g 6,553n 12,539d 529.4 x 64.7 x 34.3 feet.
Two 8-cyl. 4SCSA Burmeister & Wain-type oil engines by Harland and Wolff Ltd., Glasgow driving twin screws; 6,500 BHP, 15.5 knots.
1952: Two 7-cyl. 2SCSA oil engines by Maschinenfabrik Augsburg-Nürnberg A.G., Augsburg driving twin screws, 9,800 BHP, 15.5 knots.
6.7.1929: Launched by Wilton's Machinefabriek en Scheepswerf, Schiedam (Yard No. 318).
10.1929: Completed for Nederlandsch-Amerikaansche Stoomvaart Maatschappij, Rotterdam as DELFTDIJK.
3.9.1940: Damaged by German aircraft off Rattray Head whilst on a voyage from London to Brisbane via the north of Scotland with general cargo. Two of the crew were lost. Towed into Aberdeen Roads badly damaged. Temporary repairs carried out at Leith, and permanent repairs on the Tyne.
24.1.1950: Struck mine in the North Sea whilst on a voyage from Bremen to Vancouver.
1952: Lengthened, re-engined and renamed DONGEDYK.
1966: Sold to Chung Lien Navigation Co. S.A., Panama (Great Pacific Navigation Co. Ltd., Taipei) and renamed TUNG LONG.
12.9.1966: Arrived at Kaohsiung to be broken up.
18.2.1967: Work commenced by Cheng Lung Steel Co. Ltd.

Opposite top: *Dinteldijk* in the Mersey, 16th April 1938. *[J. and M. Clarkson]*

Opposite middle: The retreating Germans sank a number of vessels in the Nieuwe Waterweg above Maasluis in September 1944, among them the *Dinteldijk*, seen in the foreground, and the *Zuiderdam* beyond. Both were raised and scrapped, the *Zuiderdam* never having entered service. *[World Ship Photo Library collection]*

Opposite bottom: *Drechtdijk* in the Panama Canal. *[J. and M. Clarkson]*

This page: *Delftdijk* (upper) became *Dongedijk* (lower) following post-war rebuilding. *[J. and M. Clarkson and G.R. Scott collection]*

Another ship taken over by the Germans during the Second World War, the *Damsterdijk* (above) was repaired and returned to service postwar as *Dalerdijk* (below). *[Both: J. and M. Clarkson]*

As rebuildings go, those so far seen in this feature returned the ship to recognisably its previous form. Not so the work on *Diemerdijk* (above in the Thames on 31st May 1953) which transformed her into the container ship *Oriental Amiga* (below). *[Both: J. and M. Clarkson]*

4. DAMSTERDIJK/DALERDYK 1930-1963
10,155g 6,337n 490.9 x 64.7 x 34.1 feet.
1948: 10,820g 6,390n 12,450d 490.9 x 64.7 x 34.1 feet
Two 8-cyl. 4SCSA Burmeister & Wain-type oil engines by Harland and Wolff Ltd., Glasgow driving twin screws; 6,500 BHP, 14.5 knots.
1.1949: Two 6-cyl. 2SCSA oil engines by Sulzer Brothers Ltd., Winterthur driving twin screws; 8,400 BHP, 14.5 knots.
17.5.1930: Launched by Wilton's Machinefabrik and Scheepwerft, Schiedam (Yard No. 322).
9.1930: Completed for Nederlandsch-Amerikaansche Stoomvaart Maatschappij, Rotterdam as DAMSTERDIJK.
7.8.1940: Seized by German forces, becoming transport RO12 for Operation Sealion. Operated by Hamburg-Amerikanische Packetfahrt A.G., Hamburg as MULHAUSEN.
1945: Found at Kiel and returned to owners as DAMSTERDIJK.
1948: Renamed DALERDYK.
1963: Sold to Belvientos Compania Naviera S.A., Panama and renamed PRESVIA.
27.10.1963: Breaking up began at Mihara, Japan.

5. DIEMERDYK 1950-1968
11,195g 6,303n 11,780d 498.3 x 69.2 x 38.9 feet. .
Two steam turbines double-reduction geared to a single screw by General Electric Company, Erie, Pennsylvania made 1946, fitted 1950; 8,500 SHP, 16.5 knots.
17.12.1949: Launched by Wilton-Fijenoord Dok-en Werf Maats N.V., Schiedam (Yard No. 723).
6.1950: Completed for Nederlandsch-Amerikaansche Stoomvaart Maatschappij, Rotterdam as DIEMERDYK.
1968: Sold to Oriental Africa Line Inc., Monrovia (C.Y. Tung, Hong Kong) and renamed ORIENTAL AMIGA.
1973: Owners became China Maritime Trust, Taiwan (C.Y. Tung, Hong Kong) and converted to container ship.
3.1978: Laid up.
8.7.1978: Breaking up commenced by Chi Young Steel Enterprises Co Ltd, Kaohsiung.

6. DINTELDYK 1957-1970
11,366g 6,584n 11,855d 504.3 x 69.3 x 42.0 feet.
Two Pametrada steam turbines direct-reduction geared to a single screw by Wilton-Fijenoord Dok-en Werf Maatschappij N.V., Schiedam; 9,350 SHP, 16 knots.
9.6.1956: Launched by Wilton-Fijenoord Dok-en Werf Maatschappij N.V., Schiedam (Yard No. 752).
3.1957: Completed for Nederlandsch-Amerikaansche Stoomvaart Maatschappij, Rotterdam as DINTELDYK.
1970: Sold to Oriental Central America Lines Inc., Monrovia (C.Y. Tung, Hong Kong) and renamed ORIENTAL FANTASIA.
1972: Renamed HONGKONG SUCCESS.
1972: Owners became Pacific Union Lines Ltd. (C.Y. Tung), Hong Kong.
1973: Converted to carry containers.
1976: Owners became Oriental Central America Lines Inc. Monrovia (C.Y. Tung, Hong Kong).
1.1.1979: Arrived at Kaohsiung for demolition.
10.2.1979: Breaking up commenced by the Chien Tai Iron Works Co. Ltd.

Another sale to C.Y. Tung saw *Dinteldijk* (above) become *Oriental Fantasia* (below). The only change so far is to her funnel colours. *[J. and M. Clarkson]*

PUTTING THE RECORD STRAIGHT

Letters, additions, amendments and photographs relating to articles in any issues of *Record* are welcomed. Letters may be lightly edited. E-mails are welcome, but senders are asked to include their postal address.

After the Doxford gospel, the Doxford hymn

I thought this might make an interesting little piece in *Record* if more information could be discovered. You may have heard of this song which was not just sung, but also acted by five members of engine room crew, four playing the role of a piston and the fifth the scavenge pump (I think). They'd go up and down in the firing order of a Doxford engine, and singing the following song to the tune of 'MacNamara's Band':

'Well my name is William Doxford and I come from Sunderland,
I build a diesel engine, it's the finest in the land,
The side rods clang, the relief valves bang
And the fuel valves blaze away,
We're on a Doxford engine and we're bound for Swansea Bay'.

I don't know whether or not there are further verses - perhaps a reader might know and might recall the actions too?

Dr DAVID JENKINS, National Museums and Galleries of Wales, Heol Crochendy, Parc Nantgarw CF15 7QT

Preliminary research reveals that there are indeed other verses, and other versions, of the Doxford ditty, and we invite readers to submit any they know. Ed.

***Blairspey* and SC 7**

I will not comment at any length on the rest of the account (which really just suffers from an excess of journalistic enthusiasm) and concentrate on the main issue of the attack on *Blairspey.* For the record, at this stage of the war all convoy escorts were lamentably thin outside of the eastern Atlantic as there were very few long-range escorts (and no real threat from U-boats in the central or western areas). The normal practice was for a group of escorts to take an outward convoy through the danger area and then meet up with a homeward one and perform the same function in reverse. This is exactly what happened with SC 7.

The report of the master of *Blairspey,* Captain J.C. Walker, can be found at the PRO in file ADM 199/2134. The vessel was bound from Sydney, Cape Breton to Grangemouth with 1,798 standards of timber and a crew of 34 (including one marine gunner). The report categorically states that there were no casualties, and the statement in the article that the master reported 18 casualties is, I fear, completely wrong.

A summary of Walker's report is as follows:
The first torpedo struck at 10.30pm on the 18th on the port side in the way of No.1 hold about 50-60 feet from the bow. A joint blew out in the engine room at this time bringing the ship to a stop. At 1.00 am on the 19th, while the steam joint was still being repaired, the ship was torpedoed again, this time on the starboard side between Nos. 1 and 2 holds, about 100 feet from the bows. The order to abandon ship was given at this time. About five minutes later, while abandoning ship, a third torpedo hit, this one of the port side amidships about 150 feet from the bow. The boats became separated, the Master's being picked up by HMS *Bluebell* at 6.45am, the mate's by a salvage tug between 3.00 and 4.00 in the afternoon.

There is no reference to the ship breaking in two at sea, and secondary accounts suggest that the badly damaged forepart was removed after she reached the Clyde.

The salvage tug involved was the aptly named *Salvonia* (571/1939).

MALCOLM COOPER, Flat 5, Leonard Court, 68 Westbourne Terrace, London W2 3UF

The long arm of coincidence never ceases to amaze me. Only this week I had occasion to dig out my notes on the ill-fated convoy SC 7 (taken from 'Night of the U-Boats' by Paul Lund and Harry Ludlam, 1973), and had marvelled once again at the incredible rescue work carried out by the salvage tug *Salvonia.* Then lo and behold, the most excellent *Record* 22 drops on my mat, among its contents the full story of *Blairspey.*

As you point out, *Salvonia* already had on board some survivors from HX 77 (a boat load from the *Port Gisborne,* likewise from the *St Malo*), when she came upon the massacre of SC 7, only 15 of whose original 35 ships reached their destination. She then picked up 14 men from *Blairspey* (from one of two boats launched), some survivors from the *Sedgepool* (5,552/1918) and one of two boat loads from the *Clintonia* (3106/1917) before taking the *Blairspey* in tow on 19th October. The Clyde was reached on 25th October where the *Blairspey* was beached. A further 19 survivors from *Blairspey,* including Captain J.C. Walker, her master, were rescued by the corvette HMS *Bluebell,* another little ship which deserved full honours, arriving at Gourock on 20th December 1940 bursting at the seems with survivors. On a quick count I make it survivors from eight ships (but it could have been more) which also included the entire 37-man crew of the *Beatus* (3,885/1925) and complete crew (plus dog) from the Swedish *Gunborg* (1,572/1930).

At the pre-convoy conference at Sydney N.S. either Captain E. Robilliard, master of the *Creekirk* (ex-*Hyphaestos*, ex-*Milcovul*; ex-*Mariston* (3917/1912) or Captain E. William of the *Fiscus* (4815/1928), had gloomily remarked to another skipper along the lines of 'If we get a tin fish this trip that's it. With what I've got on board we'll go down like a stone!' It makes little odds which master mariner saw so accurately into the future since both ships were torpedoed and sank with the loss of all hands, like stones, before anyone even had the chance to leap over the wall into the sea. *Creekirk* had a very nasty cargo indeed when taking her chances of surviving into account: 5,900 tons of iron ore plus, in just one hold, an unquoted tonnage of sheet steel. *Fiscus*, which had straggled before she was hit, had steel ingots and crated aircraft.

D.H. JOHNZON, 53 West Avenue, Filey Y014 9AX

Netherlands reader Chris Kleiss kindly supplied a copy of a postcard which helps confirm that the photograph of Blairspey *on page 120 of Record 22 is indeed at Huelva. Ed.*

A bit on the side

Just received *Record* 22 - another very enjoyable issue, although must admit that offshore support vessels cannot be described as things of beauty, and who chooses their names? I have seen many peculiar names, but *Safe Truck* ranks amongst the most odd!

Regarding the issue of rotating pages, I have absolutely no trouble in this regard, it is as you say a small price to pay when doing so does justice to such a stunning picture as that of *War Climax* on the last page. The detail in this photograph is exceptional, and can only be appreciated as a 'landscape' format. Please stick to this format wherever you can.

Regarding things of beauty, I have a soft spot for the Empire F type, they had a kind of charm that came with a defiant ugliness and utility. They had a character all of their own - I wish that they were still around as an antidote to car carriers and container ships!

TONY SMYTHE, 35 Avondale Road, Rayleigh, Essex SS6 8NJ

The many replies received have been supportive of our policy of rotating good photos to fill a 'landscape' page. Ed.

Loch up the caption writer

Despite evidence from the photographs he was captioning, the editor seems to have been convinced that Loch Ryan *was called* Loch Avon, *and wrongly named the ship on pages 71 and 75 of* Record 22. *He has since revisited his optician. Apologies to author of the article David Burrell and thanks to Alan Phipps and others for pointing this out.*

Turner, Brightman

Our photo feature on Turner, Brightman ships in Record 22 *stimulated considerable interest, and we will publish a follow up in a forthcoming* Record.

Sperrbrechers

Reading the letters in *Record* 21 I note the comments about *Tower Crown* and her career as a German minesweeper. Peter Arndt's 'Deutsche Sperrbrecher 1914-1945' states she was only ever *Sperrbrecher III, Hilfsperrbrecher C* and *Sperrbrecher C.* He shows *Sperrbrecher A* as being the *Waldtraut Horn* (3,995/1928). Karl-Heinz Schwadtke in 'Deutschlands Handelsschiffe 1939-1945' shows the *Robert Bornhofen* as being *Sperrbrecher III,* then *Sperrbrecher A* and *Sperrbrecher 14.* Arndt has *Sperrbrecher 14* as being the *Bockenheim* (7,019/1920). Who is correct? I am inclined to go with Arndt as his work is a specialist one on the sperrbrechers.

DAVID BURRELL, 63 Avisyard Avenue, Cumnock, Ayrshire KA18 3BJ.

'Delighted' is hardly strong enough to show how pleased the editors are to be able to publish this photograph of *Tower Crown* as a *Sperrbrecher* (top). See the accompanying letter from David Burrell. *[Nigel Farrell collection]*

Dennis Johnzon sent the shot of the Chilean-owned *Flora* awaiting the breakers at Briton Ferry in the summer of 1956 (middle). She was shown in *Record* 21 on page 64 of the Cornelis Nieuwland article as *Stad Haarlem. [A. Duncan]*

Ivor Rooke was interested by *Oyarzun* on page 59 of the Nieuwland feature, and provided this photograph of the ship under its original name, *White Jacket* of George Hallett, Cardiff (bottom). Comparison of the two shots reveals many similarities forward, but not the fidded masts seen in the Nieuwland photograph. More difficult to explain is that the 80-foot raised quarterdeck is not obvious in the view of *White Jacket. [Ivor Rooke collection]*

Points from the past

Herewith a few observations on past issues.

Record 3 page 185. The lower photo depicts *Colebrooke* berthed in Trafalgar Dock, East Side, Liverpool - not Clarence Dock. Behind the transit sheds Clarence Dock power station can be seen which was built on the site of the Clarence Dock. In the ensuing reconstruction the new Trafalgar Dock evolved on the site of the Clarence Half Tide Dock - with the original Trafalgar Dock becoming Trafalgar Branch Dock. The only sections of Clarence Dock that remained at the time the photo was taken were the two graving docks, Numbers 1 and 2 (as indeed they still thankfully do today) and they now currently mark the southern extremity of the Mersey Docks and Harbour Company's commercial dock estate. *Brookmount* in the photo on page 181 is also shown on the same berth.

Record 3 page 167. The steam barge *Decempedes* continued in service with Imperial Chemical Industries (Mond Division) Ltd. on the Mersey Estuary even longer than your caption to the photo suggests. She carried her last ICI cargo in February1968 and was scrapped by Routledge Brothers at Garston Beach on the Upper Mersey during 1969 (q.v. *Sea Breezes,* October 1969, No. 286 page 647. As correctly pointed out she was a motor barge by this time having been converted in 1957. However, upon demolition of the hull her 125 BHP Thornycroft diesel was subsequently installed in the small motor launch/tug *Annie Sea* which was based at Liverpool.

Record 17 page 46. *Derbyshire,* as stated in *Record* 18 page 46, the caption is wrong - but for a different reason - the date should read 22nd May 1976 not June. I know - I also witnessed her arrival on the New Waterway that day! This must have been one of - if not the - last voyage under Bibby Line ownership, as by August 27th that year she was reported arrived in Montreal already under her new name of *Captain Lygnos* following sale to Greeks.

NIGEL BOWKER, 9 Poulton Green Close, Spital, Bebington, Wirral, Merseyside, CH63 9FS.

Tweaking 22

Page 74. *Lochkatrine* and *Lochgoil:* the Royal Mail Steam Packet Company was never Ltd. but was incorporated by Royal Charter, like P&O and PSNC. The name is correctly given in the heading.

Page 75. *Lochavon:* there is no doubt that this photo was taken of the vessel on her trials in the Clyde. One has only to look at the houseflag at the mainmast which is that of Harland and Wolff, rather than the Royal Mail flag. The only occasion when this flag would be flown at sea would have been on the vessel's trials before she was handed over to her owners.

Page 87. *Zingara:* perhaps it could have been made clearer that her French purchasers in 1927 kept her name and that she didn't become *Djena* until resold in 1930.

Page 86. *Zillah:* I think she was sunk on 22nd October 1917, not September.

BILL LAXON, Waimarama, Upper Whangateau Road, PO Box 171, Matakana 1240, New Zealand.

Of sheer strakes, rolled plates and a comatose cat

This concerns a caption note to a photograph of the *Orsova* on page 211, *Record* 20 in the very interesting article about the Nile Steam Ship Co. Ltd. by David Burrell. You make the comment that the photograph clearly shows that the bulwarks were set in from the side. This is undeniably true; but so are the rails of the *Naess Talisman* on the opposite page, the *Clerk-Maxwell* on page 212 and probably all four ships illustrated on page 213. Some, usually smaller, ships have had rails and even the superstructure set in because they were expected to enter narrow locks or bridge cuttings where even a slight list could cause an overhang to one side and possibly result in damage. But I don't think this was the case with the captioned ships where it is most likely to be caused by the nature of the sheer strake.

In traditional steel ship construction the sheer strake projected above the adjacent deck stringer and the two were bonded together by an angle bar, welded or riveted. In this case the rails or bulwarks would extend directly above the sheer strake. For various reasons an alternative came into vogue in the 1950s and 1960s for larger ships. This involved a rolled plate, welded to deck stringer and sheer strake instead of the costly angle construction. The rails or bulwarks were then set inboard of the rolled section above a gutter bar. Post-war naval ships had a similar arrangement but without the gutter bar, designed to ensure that radioactive or toxic matter could be washed overboard as soon as possible.

As if to prove that there is little that is truly new, I think that rolled iron sections were used by Brunel on his famous *Great Britain.* Riveted to the deck stringer and sheer strake it must have provided a stronger feature than an angle construction at that point.

Two points from recent issues - no problems with the length of the Ellerman articles, it would be interesting to have a similar feature in due course, about another company, naturally. Equally, no problems with 'rotating pages'. The only objections were from the cat who was apparently comatose on my lap until I rotated the magazine. Dry cleaning will probably sort out the blood stains.

KEN GARRETT, 3 The Grange, East Malling, Kent ME19 6AH

SOURCES AND ACKNOWLEDGEMENTS

Photographs are from the collection of John Clarkson unless otherwise credited. We thank all who gave permission for their photographs to be used, and for help in finding photographs we are particularly grateful to Tony Smith, Jim McFaul and David Whiteside of the World Ship Photo Library; to Ian Farquhar, Bill Laxon, Peter Newall, Ivor Rooke, William Schell, George Scott; to David Hodge and Bob Todd of the National Maritime Museum; Dr. David Jenkins of the National Museums and Galleries of Wales; and other museums and institutions listed.

Research sources have included the *Registers* of William Schell and Tony Starke, *Lloyd's Register, Lloyd's Confidential Index, Lloyd's War Losses, Mercantile Navy Lists,* and *Marine News.* Use of the facilities of the World Ship Society's Central Record, the Guildhall Library, the Public Record Office and Lloyd's Register of Shipping are gratefully acknowledged. Particular thanks also to William Schell and John Bartlett for various information, to Heather Fenton for editorial and indexing work, and to Marion Clarkson for accountancy services.

Bergen Line

Thanks to Laurence Dunn, Ambrose Greenway, Ian Rae and Soren Thørsoe. Books consulted were:

Dag Bakka Junior, *Bergenske, Byen og Selskapet,* Seagull Publishing, Bergen, 1993.

Ambrose Greenway *A Century of North Sea Passenger Steamers,* Ian Allan, Shepperton, 1986

Finns in the fifties

Thanks to Bengt Sjöström who read the draft of the text and made a number of helpful suggestions.

Four sailing barges

Much of the technical information has been taken from Ken Garrett's book, R. Lapthorn and Co. Ltd., published by Ships in Focus during 2001, with the addition of information that has come to light since publication. Some of the information about Eastwoods Ltd. has been gleaned from 'Bricks and Brickies' written by Frank Willmott and published privately in 1972. A good friend, Bob Childs, to whom is extended warmest thanks, supplied most of the additional notes.

HELP PUT IT ON RECORD

On hand for publication is an excellent article by James Pottinger on the whale catchers built in Germany in 1936 and 1937 for Lord Leverhulme's Southern Whaling and Sealing Company. Unfortunately, photographs of these vessels have proved totally elusive, and we are appealing to readers for the loan of, or information about the location of, any shots of the following, under any names:

Southern Barrier later *Kos 29.*

Southern Breeze later *Gascoyne.*

Southern Floe.

Southern Gem.

Southern Isles later *Uni 2.*

Southern Maid later *Uni 3.*

Southern Sea later *Uni 4.*

The whale catchers served with the South African Navy during the Second World War and all but the lost *Southern Floe* continued in civilian service until the 1960s.

QUEENSLAND-BRASILIA STAR

Captain A.W. Kinghorn

Nothing if not versatile, ever ready to adapt to any service within the Vestey Group's normal trading, Blue Star Line of London achieved something of a reputation for changing their ships' names with what - to those not in the know - seemed almost dizzying frequence. Their four main lines - Liverpool's Lamport and Holt and Booth Lines, Austasia Line of Singapore, together with Blue Star itself - voyaged regularly on liner trades ranging from the U.K/Europe to North and South America, South and East Africa, Australia, New Zealand, Middle and Far East and the Pacific Islands, with a few places in between. To serve these trades they had a pool of around forty versatile vessels - fine ships, mostly able to carry refrigerated cargo as well as general. To keep pace with various requirements a ship would be taken up from one trade and placed on another, with appropriate name change if deemed desirable. Thus, *Queensland Star* became the *Brasilia Star* on 9th June 1972 while I stood by her as master in Cardiff Docks. The steel name letters were burned off at bow and stern, replaced with the new ones, neatly cut and welded in place. Port of registry London remained the same. The old name letters were carefully retained for future re-use.

A new class of ship

One of that rather classy series built in the late 1950s for the proposed chilled beef trade between Queensland and the UK, *Queensland Star* was a 1957 product of Glasgow's Fairfield Shipbuilding and Engineering Co Ltd, their yard number 779. Of 10,657 tons gross on an overall length of 511' 6", she had five hatches - three forward of the bridge, two abaft in what for the past twenty years had been the usual manner.

Her total cargo capacity comprised 584,692 cubic feet of which 391,892 was refrigeratable, the remaining 192,800 general cargo space. With her class sisters, she had five masts - fore, main (which carried the topmast), mizzen, jigger and spanker. Although of course in 1957 these masts were not rigged with sails they continued the old nomenclature. Propulsion was provided by twin five-cylinder Doxfords, a happy combination which drove her along effortlessly at well over 16 knots.

With British master and officers she had a large Singapore Chinese crew. Six passengers could be accommodated under the bridge in comfortable en-suite cabins - her most distinguished regular passenger to and from visiting her Australian relatives was H.R.H. Princess Alice who expressed a preference for this ship with the relaxed, no-nonsense atmosphere and excellent catering provided. When, eventually, Queensland chilled beef did not come up to expectations - due to uncooperative Australian weather over several seasons - the ship was placed in other trades, at first retaining her original name. But when Blue Star Line's prestigious 25-year-old regular cargo passenger liners were withdrawn from the UK-East coast of South American service, *Queensland Star,* at the time unloading Tasmanian apples in Cardiff, was renamed *Brasilia Star* (with an 's' as that is how the new Brazilian capital city spelt its name).

Changed trade, changed name

My duty in Cardiff at that time included responsibility also for the *Southland Star,* still a twin-heavy-Stulcken-derrick break-bulk cargo liner. She and her sister *New Zealand Star* were in 1967 the last two conventional cargo liners the company built, converted to cellular container ships at their Bremer Vulkan builder's yard ten years later. But this conversion was still well in the future and now she also was

The *Queensland Star* of 1957. . .

in with Tasmanian fruit. With both ships berthed on either side of the dock I spent an interesting ten days walking between the two daily, dealing with both ships' paperwork amongst other matters. *Southland Star's* British crew had paid off and mostly gone home, but to obtain permission for *Queensland Star's* Singapore Chinese crew to buy duty free cigarettes from the ship's bond (even though they were not officially entitled on a ship 'Off Articles'), I had to put on my persuasive best with the Cardiff Customs officers. An important part of any ship captain's job is to look after his crew and in those days lack of duty-free cigarettes was considered a severe deprivation! Later in the voyage I sometimes wondered why I had bothered.

Late one afternoon the Harbour Master came aboard, telling me to shift ship along the quay that evening to allow room for an expected arrival. Berthed on the outer harbour wall we had no engines at that short notice (the chief having a big survey job on). I had on board a few Chinese sailors (most had gone ashore), an excellent Scottish chief officer and one cadet; a bare minimum required for this kind of manoeuvre, which is known as warping. We had to shift a couple of ship-lengths ahead. The most important thing in this evolution with an offshore wind is to ensure you never let all your ropes go at the same time - otherwise you will drift across the dock with no engines and may consequently get into all sorts of trouble. I would be on the bridge controlling the manoeuvre by walkie-talkie. The chief officer forward knew exactly what to do, pass the lines ahead one at a time to the men onshore - use ship's windlass and winches to heave her ahead - have both anchors ready to let go should all ropes be accidentally let go at once. The cadet, who had never done this before, would be in charge of handling the ropes to the quay aft, so we showed him what to do using small ship-models. Despite an increasingly gusty offshore wind and thanks to the chief officer's and cadet's perspicacity, we shifted along the quay without mishap, for which I was thankful.

New maiden voyage

When we came to sail on 14th June on our 'maiden' voyage the pilot said what a pleasure it was to take a 'real ship' out, compared with some of the nautical monstrosities he had to deal with these days. And so we sailed in ballast for Buenos Aires, a pleasant passage made in 15 days at 17.7 knots in mainly fine weather. No passengers were carried as the last of the River Plate Boats (as they were called) were still running. Entering the River Plate we passed one of these, the outbound *Brasil Star,* on her last voyage before heading for Taiwan breakers. *Brasilia* meeting *Brasil* for the first and last time was surely an occasion and her captain kindly

Brasil Star

gave me the latest port info by VHF telephone. I was new to command on this run and his tips of do's and don'ts was much appreciated.

Berthing at Buenos Aires on 1st July we loaded frozen lamb while observing the usual tense political situation prevailing ashore there. One night walking back to the ship after a pleasant evening I found myself crossing a spacious well-kept lawn near a large, imposing building (which I later realised was the army barracks). A succession of whistles announced my approach whereupon I suddenly observed, standing around the walls, a long line of khaki-clad, German-style-steel-helmeted soldiers slowly raising their rifles at me. Raising my hands in best Hollywood Western style I retraced my steps, greatly relieved when the whistles again blew and the guards stamped their rifle butts on the ground, resuming their original stance.

River Plate tragedy

Sailing down the Plate to Montevideo five days later we passed the burned out hulk of the *Royston Grange,* alongside there now after her disastrous collision in the Plate with the Taiwan tanker *Tan Chi,* which resulted in a fire killing every single man in the *Royston Grange* and most of those in the *Tan Chi.* Cause of the collision was thought afterwards to have been interaction between the steep-sided banks of the dredged channel as the two vessels approached each other, causing them to collide, igniting the fatal spark which set off a fireball in the presumably not-gasfree tanker.

Royston Grange was now completely devoid of

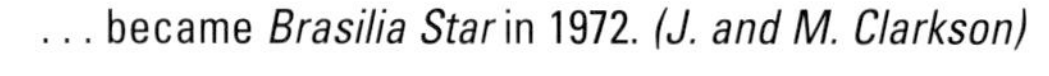

. . . became *Brasilia Star* in 1972. *(J. and M. Clarkson)*

GLADSTONE STAR

TOWNSVILLE STAR

Shown here in the order of building, the *Queensland Star* and her near-sisters show some interesting differences, probably resulting from different interpretations of the design by the three shipyards involved. The *Queensland Star* (opposite page, top in June 1969) and the Cammell, Laird-built *Rockhampton Star* (this page) are alike in having solid crosstrees, but show minor differences in their superstructures, and the height of the masts aft. The *Rockhampton Star* lacks the radar scanner perched rather incongruously on her funnel, but other shots show she eventually received it. Her hull colour varied from black through lavender to pale grey during her Blue Star career, which ended in 1981 when she became the Panama-flag *Golden Lady.* She was broken up in Bangladesh in 1983.

The Bremer Vulkan-built pair, *Gladstone Star* (opposite middle) and *Townsville Star* (opposite bottom), were significantly longer, at 539 feet, but externally seem similar to *Queensland Star* apart from their distinctively-different cross trees and a shorter forecastle. *Gladstone Star* was sold in 1982 and with her named shortened to *Gladys* went to breakers at Gadani Beach later that year. *Townsville Star* was sold directly to breakers at Kaohsiung in 1980.

The builders seem to have been allowed their choice of engines, the Vegesack-built pair having ten-cylinder M.A.N. diesels, the *Queensland Star* two five-cylinder Doxfords built under licence by Fairfield, and the *Rockhampton Star* an eight-cylinder Burmeister & Wain engine built by Harland and Wolff. *[Opposite top: F.W. Hawks; others J. and M. Clarkson]*

paint, her brown rusted steelwork only relieved by the aluminium Maltese cross on her tall Houlder Line funnel (see the photograph on page 133 of *Record* 19). Torn open bows and festooned anchor cables told how she had hit the tanker head on. Awestruck by this unforgettably fearful sight, I had our ensign dipped in silent tribute as we moved slowly past her to our berth.

We were in and out of Montevideo in 13 hours during which time our agent showed me the amendment made to the white sandstone seafront Battle of the River Plate Memorial on which were now engraved - as well as British names - those of the German sailors killed in that action, an addition few would question as the pocket battleship *Graf Spee's* honourable Captain Langsdorf ensured that no British merchant seamen were killed in his 1939 attacks upon our shipping.

Crew trouble

Two days in Santos (10th to 12th June) had us loading frozen lamb and cartons of tinned coffee (Nescafã´). It was in Santos that the chief officer decided he had a much-needed chance to paint right round the ship's grey hull. Unfortunately our Chinese crew had proved themselves temperamentally and physically unsuitable for this hardworking South American service. One night at sea I was called down to the crew accommodation to quell a knife fight between recalcitrant seamen. My sudden appearance in full uniform gave them pause for thought and two knives were meekly handed over to me - but how can you trust fellows like that? They had, perhaps, been spoiled on their previous long, leisurely Australian voyages where unworked overtime payment was generous. But here they had to work hard tending cargo gear, shifting hatch beams and heavy, old fashioned insulated hatch plugs at every deck in every port as rapid loading proceeded, really earning their wages. And when the chief officer gave them this painting job they replied 'No Can Do!' (not, they demanded, without at least double overtime pay plus a bonus.) 'O.K.' said our big Scots chief officer calmly, 'No more overtime for you lot,' and he and the two cadets proceeded to paint round the entire ship in two days. As the sailors depended on their overtime payments for spending money they lost face with their engine room and catering shipmates - and more importantly, lost cash - and pleaded to be allowed to resume work. But we were adamant. At the end of the voyage that Chinese crew was replaced with a good British crew who were quite prepared to work as required.

Homeward bound

We were in and out of next port Rio de Janeiro in one day. Not, however, before the local customs officers had helped themselves to much of the contents of our bonded and food storerooms. This type of procedure was new to me, but I learned it was just 'a custom of the port'. The old steamer *Dunedin Star* (1950/7,322), of which I had been chief officer eleven years earlier and was now Lamport and Holt's *Roland* (see *Record* 9) was putting to sea that evening and we exchanged three prolonged blasts on our whistles as she moved slowly past, out into the night.

Having satisfied the Rio Customs officers'

requirements, homeward bound across the Atlantic was non-eventful, until fog beset us as we approached the Bay of Biscay. Fitful fog, the kind you keep thinking is going to lift soon but which goes on and on - up past Cape Finisterre, across the Bay and round Ushant into the English Channel where shipping traffic became denser and denser, unseen by human eye, only visible on our radar. I hoped we had this rather old set tuned in sufficiently to see everything, including the numerous small fishing boats crossing our path. Fortunately it seemed we had.

The deck officers each kept their four-hour bridge watches with the duty cadet, staring into the gloom around us and the radar alternately, changing over every fifteen minutes to provide a little essential variety. I as master of the vessel remained on the bridge for the three days and nights the fog lasted, occasionally taking a brief rest on my bridge sea cabin bunk when visibility improved during the chief officer's 4 to 8 watches, always ready for a call if visibility deteriorated.

I was impressed how well Channel shipping was disciplined, keeping to the newly ordained traffic lanes and proceeding at a safe, moderate speed - all slowing down when fog grew denser, speeding up in clearer patches. In the eastern end of the Channel visibility improved, giving a perfectly clear sun-washed morning in Dover Strait and up to the Hook of Holland. In the narrow sea lanes here, bordered by channel marking buoys, there is little room to manoeuvre at the 'crossroads' and when a Russian cargo ship overtook us I had no option but to stop engines, enabling the hammer and sickle to forge past - even though an overtaking vessel is required to avoid the vessel she is overtaking. I realised however, as she sped past, that earlier that morning. I had overtaken her, which put her in the clear. The Rule of the Road at Sea is unambiguous and simply requires every ship to avoid collision.

On arrival alongside in Rotterdam I was handed the usual sheaf of shipping papers and magazines, in one of which the front page advertisement showed a similar ship to ours, telling 'She's made a good passage this trip, thanks to so-and-so's lubricating oils!' (clearly she did not get into fog!) Even so we had made our 5,258-mile passage from Rio at an average speed of 16.19 knots - including several days steaming much slower than this in the fog. It had, for me, been a highly educational voyage.

I went home from Rotterdam on 1st August leaving the ship to carry on, henceforth manned by a totally British crew. By no means all Singapore Chinese crews were as bad as this lot, but the time had come for a change and with air fares to and from Singapore now a serious consideration, a British crew was deemed preferable. Her name fluctuated between *Queensland Star* and *Brasilia Star* until 1979 when - superceded by container shipping - she went to Kaohsiung breakers at the early age of 22.

A final look at *Brasilia Star.* She carried this name from 1972 until 1975, when she reverted to *Queensland Star,* and from 1978 until 1979 when she was sold to Taiwan for scrap.

FOUR SAILING BARGES

Ken Garrett

When collecting photographs for my recent history of R. Lapthorn and Co. Ltd., John Clarkson helpfully sent me these four lovely photographs of spritsail barges, all taken in the 1930s and apparently off Leigh-on-Sea. For one reason or another they were not thought appropriate for the book but being far too good to file and forget, I delved a little into the history of each vessel before they were purchased and cut down to motor barges by Lapthorns. The results of the research and some additional notes follow.

ALICE MAY No.2 in 1899 and No.9 in 1957 in Ipswich.
O.N. 109205 89.17g 69.9n 89.0 x 20.5 x 6.9 feet.
12.5.1899: Completed by W.B. MacLearon, Harwich for Robert J. Smith, Trimley as ALICE MAY.
5.10.1927: Sold to R. and W. Paul Ltd., Ipswich.
25.11.1949: Sold to John Anthony Lapthorn, Hoo and converted into a houseboat.
25.11.1956: Acquired by R. Lapthorn and Co. Ltd., Hoo.
1957: Re-commissioned and fitted with a 4-cyl. 4SA oil engine made by F. Perkins Ltd., Peterborough.
14.3.1966: Sold to A. Jemmett, Faversham.
10.3.1970: Sold to Mrs. V. Plummer, Camberwell. Later abandoned in the West India Dock, London and sank alongside. Lifted onto quayside in the Blackwall Basin and used by the Sea Scouts.
1982: Broken up, but register not closed until 1999.

The photograph from July 1937 shows *Alice May* with all her sails furled but it is hard to determine whether she is at anchor or not. Maybe the skipper and mate for'ard have just raised the anchor or are preparing to let it go. At any rate, her rig is clearly that of a mulie with a gaff-rigged mizzen. She had a calamity in her early days when she sank at anchor in the Lower Hope after being struck by the steamer *Denmark.* It happened in December 1899 when she was carrying a cargo of empty bottles from Dunkirk. It all sounds very dramatic and doubtless it was for all concerned, but unfortunately it was quite a regular occurrence in those days. Many, like the *Alice May,* were raised, repaired and soon back at work again.

She had a busy year in 1909 when she made 30 voyages under the command of Frederick Strange. She carried coal from Hull to Ipswich and Felixstowe and returned north with grain from an importer in Harwich. Earlier, she had been involved in carrying scrap and pig iron to Bentall's Foundry in Heybridge Basin.

When first bought by Tony Lapthorn she was converted into a houseboat and moored at Hoo. She also served as his company office and until just recently the registered office was still known as *Alice May.* Some parts of her were salvaged when she was broken up and were given to the Museum of London in Docklands.

ETHEL No.1 in 1894 and No.4 in 1955 in Harwich.
O.N. 99453 83.80g 72.51n 82.4 x 19.7 x 6.95 feet.
8.3.1894: Completed by J and H. Cann, Harwich for Joseph W. Holmes (22/64), Ipswich, Joseph L. Holmes (26/64), Harwich and William Green (16/64), Grays as ETHEL.
27.5.1921: Sold to Walter Ellis, Ipswich.
19.7.1928: Sold to Cranfield Brothers Ltd., Ipswich.
21.10.1955: Registered *de novo* after being fitted with a 3-cyl. 4SA Kelvin oil engine made by The Bergius Co. Ltd., Glasgow.
1.2.1972: Sold to Silvertown Services Lighterage Ltd., London.
8.6.1972: Chartered to Gestetner Duplicators Ltd., London and renamed DAVID GESTETNER.
20.11.1974: Sold to Tate and Lyle Group Ltd., London and renamed ETHEL.
13.4.1977: Re-engined with a 6-cyl 4SA oil engine made by Detroit Diesel, Allison Division, General Motors Corp, Detroit, USA.
5.9.1978: Sold to Arnot Butchart Investments Ltd., Toronto, Canada.
1992: Lying dis-masted and dilapidated at New London, Connecticut, U.S.A.

Like many another, *Ethel* was registered *de novo,* as the Customs Registrars described it, when the barge was re-registered after having an engine fitted. With sailing barges it is particularly important to record the Port Registration Numbers for identification purposes because so many of them were built and registered when there were no restrictions. This *Ethel* was not the same *Ethel L* that became Lapthorn's *Pride Of Sheppey.* Frequently there were a number of craft of the same name on the British Register quite apart from the same port. Sometimes these registrations were made very close together. For example; *Sirdar,* O.N. 110009, No. 222 in 1898 in London and *Sirdar,* O.N. 110033, No. 248 in 1898 in London. That is quite an unusual name, imagine the proliferation of *Elizabeths* and *Victorias.*

This *Ethel* was always considered to be of exceptionally heavy construction despite which she had a slight twist thought to have been sustained in the Kentish Stour at Sandwich. Photographed in February 1937, her cargo looks to be bags of flour, sheeted over, from Ipswich, probably for Strood or Winchester Wharf just above Cannon Street Railway Bridge. Bags of flour, probably weighing at least one hundredweight, would be difficult to stow in the close confines of a barge's hold making a deck cargo a possibility to get the maximum permissible deadweight.

Following the success of the *May* (57/1891) as a promotional venture during the Montreal Olympic Games in 1976, Tate and Lyle decided to repeat the operation with the *Ethel.* She motored to Antwerp where she was loaded aboard a cargo ship owned by Federal Commerce and Navigation Ltd. of Montreal. The cradle used for the trip was the same as used for the *May* but modified for slightly different dimensions. She sailed around the Great Lakes and down the eastern seaboard of the USA and even ventured as far as Nassau in the Bahamas. She was last reported in 1992 in a dilapidated condition alongside at New London in Connecticut. There have been some rumours that her lines had been taken off and a replica built in steel but I have no confirmation.

MILDREDA No.100 in 1900 and No.62 in 1951 in London.
O.N. 112722 76.19g 61.42n 84.8 x 19.5 x 6.3 feet.
22.6.1900: Completed by Horace Shrubsall, Ipswich for Matthew Mildred (21/64), Philip Augustus Morris (22/64) and Albert Edward Jenner (21/64), Bankside as MILDREDA.
12.9.1900: Sold to joint owners Wakeley Brothers Ltd., Philip A. Morris and Albert E. Jenner, Bankside.
25.2.1918: Sold to Horace Shrubsall, East Greenwich.
18.10.1920: Sold to James D. Watson, Little Wakering,
17.1.1921: Cecil Edward Gilders (16/64), Leigh-on-Sea became part owner.
17.12.1923: On the death of J.D. Watson, joint owners became Fanny Rose Watson, Little Wakering; Violet Boosey, Maldon; George Jonathan Watson, Little Wakering and Douglas George Verney, Southend-on-Sea.
20.11.1944: Sold to Alfred George Wood, Sittingbourne.
22.3.1945: Sold to Paul Carden, Wakes Colne.
24.6.1946: Sold to Stanley Underdown, Queenborough and Thomas William Schmid, Sheerness.
26.6.1950: Thomas William Schmid, Queenborough became sole owner.
3.10.1950: Sold to George Andrews and Son (Freightage) Ltd., Sittingbourne.
20.3.1951: Sold to joint owners Leslie G. Strevens, Harold E. Andrews and Royden W. Andrews, Sittingbourne. Registered *de novo* when fitted with a 4-cyl. 4SA oil engine made in 1946 by the Atlantic Engine Co. Ltd., Wishaw.
17.1.1953: Joint owners became Harold E. Andrews and Leslie G. Strevens, Sittingbourne.
16.8.1954: Sold to Rachel P. Lapthorn, Hoo and re-engined with a 6-cyl. 4SA oil engine made by the Chrysler Corporation, Detroit, USA.
21.12.1954: Sold to R. Lapthorn and Co. Ltd., Hoo.
30.12.1956: Stranded across Faversham Creek with a cargo of superphosphate and declared a constructive total loss.
22.12.1970: Registry closed. Broken up by the owner.

An estuary topsail barge, the October 1936 photograph clearly shows *Mildreda* at anchor. Her chaffcutter steering wheel is plainly visible. There has always been a bit of mystery concerning her early life; she was thought to have been built for racing and was certainly thought of as a fast barge but nevertheless was sold after a few months 'owing to a dispute'. Maybe her performance did not come up to expectation although she came third in the Thames match and second in the Medway match in 1900. Perhaps the dispute involved her cargo carrying capacity.

She was considered to have been built on the light side and in later years was described by bargemen as a 'watercress bed'. In other words she leaked and had water running through all the time.

Later owners, George Andrews, his son Harold and adopted son Leslie Strevens were associated with Sully Brothers and carried out some technical supervision for them. They also pooled the earnings of some of their barges.

LANCASHIRE No.115 in 1900 and No.246 in 1954 in London.
O.N. 112734 53.24g 43.20n 78.6 x 17.1 x 5.0 feet.
11.7.1900: Completed by Alfred M. White, Teynham for Eastwood and Co. Ltd., Lambeth as LANCASHIRE.
25.6.1943: Sold to Wakeley Brothers and Co. Ltd., Bankside.
27.7.1953: Sold to Rachel P. Lapthorn, Hoo.
7.12.1954: Registered *de novo* when fitted with a 6-cyl. 4SA oil engine made by the Chrysler Corporation, Detroit, USA. Owners became R. Lapthorn and Co. Ltd., Hoo.
17.4.1955: Damaged by fire at No.2 Jetty, Beckton, not repaired and used as a loading pontoon near Herring Point, Heybridge. Later, buried in a landfill site near Maldon Hythe.

A river topsail barge, the photographs from August 1934 show *Lancashire* under full sail but running light with no cargo. She was one of a group of twenty barges built for Eastwoods with county names. Her topsail proudly proclaims her owner's name. The company had been established as builder's merchants in Lambeth in the early 1800s, gradually they built up a fleet of sailing barges and by 1880 they had taken over a number of brick works in Kent. Their base was at Wellington Wharf, more or less the site of the present Festival Hall. Later they expanded with brick works elsewhere, cement works and coal depots as far afield as Sussex and Lincolnshire. Eastwoods canal barges took cement for the building of Wembley Stadium in the early 1920s; one wonders how the cement will get to the new stadium project. Eastwoods were absorbed into the Redland Group in 1963.

Naturally the barge would have been involved in carrying the company's bricks from Otterham Quay, Lower Halstow and Conyer. Fully laden, *Lancashire* could carry between 38 and 44,000 bricks and the freight rate in 1912 from Sittingbourne to London Bridge was three shillings and twopence farthing per 1,000 bricks. She would also have carried cement and coal. She was purchased by Wakeley Brothers during the war and carried much ballast and Kentish ragstone for building up the Essex sea walls. Finally, she became a constructive total loss with a cargo of fertilizer and was purchased by Tony Lapthorn. He cut all the gear away, repaired her, installed an engine and traded her as a motor barge for a short while before she again ran out of luck and had a fire at Beckton.